# EDGAR CAYCE'S ESP

# A.R.E. MEMBERSHIP SERIES

EDGAR CAYCE'S ESP

by Kevin J. Todeschi
and the
Editors of the A.R.E.

ASSOCIATION FOR
RESEARCH AND
ENLIGHTENMENT

A.R.E. Press • Virginia Beach • Virginia

A.R.E. Press
Sixty-Eighth & Atlantic Avenue
P.O. Box 656
Virginia Beach, VA 23451-0656

Todeschi, Kevin J.
    Edgar Cayce's ESP / by Kevin J. Todeschi and the editors of the A.R.E.
        p.    cm. — (A.R.E. membership series : 3)
    ISBN 0-87604-374-0
    1. Cayce, Edgar, 1877-1945.  2. Parapsychology—Case studies.  I. Association for Research and Enlightenment.  II. Title.  III. Series.
BF1027.C3T63    1996
133.8'092—dc21                                96-329226

## The *A.R.E. Membership Series*

This book, *Edgar Cayce's ESP*, is the third in a continuing series of books that is published by the Association for Research and Enlightenment, Inc., for individuals who are especially interested in their personal and spiritual growth and transformation.

The A.R.E. was founded in 1931 as a nonprofit organization to study, research, and disseminate information on ESP, dreams, holistic health, meditation, and life after death. The A.R.E. continues its mission today, nurturing a worldwide membership with conferences, study groups, and a variety of publications—all aimed at helping seekers find paths that will lead to a more fulfilling life, mentally, physically, and spiritually. The hallmark of A.R.E.'s publications is to be helpful and hopeful. A.R.E. is committed to assisting in personal growth and making available nourishing entertainment.

Many of the books published by A.R.E. are available in bookstores throughout the world and all are available directly from the A.R.E.'s mail-order catalogs.

Three new books in this *A.R.E. Membership Series* are sent at no cost each year to individuals who are Sponsoring members or Life members of A.R.E. Each of the titles in this series will become available, one year after initial publication, for purchase by individuals throughout the world who are interested in individual growth and transformation.

For more information about membership benefits of the nonprofit Association for Research and Enlightenment, Inc., please turn to the last page in this volume.

## The A.R.E. Membership Series:

# Contents

# INTRODUCTION

Since 1901, the information in the Edgar Cayce readings has been explored by individuals from every imaginable background and discipline. In addition to individuals from all walks and stations of life, this vast scope of materials has come to the attention of educators, historians, theologians, medical professionals, and scientists. No doubt, part of the attraction has been that regardless of the field of study, Cayce has continually proven himself years ahead of his time. Decades ago, he was emphasizing the importance of diet, attitudes, emotions, exercise, and the patient's role—physically, mentally, and spiritually—in the treatment of illness. As a result, he has been called "the father of holistic medicine" and has been recognized for describing the workings of the human body and foreseeing the direction of health care.

In the field of psychology, he has often been compared to Carl Jung. In the realm of education, he stands with Rudolf Steiner. Dr. Richard H. Drummond, one of the world's most renowned theological scholars, has called the Cayce information on spirituality "the finest devotional material of the 20th century."

In history, the Cayce readings gave insights into Judaism that were verified a decade after his death. In world affairs, he saw the collapse of communism nearly fifty years before it happened. Even in the field of physics, a professor and fellow of the American Physical Society theorized a connection between the elementary-particle theory and the way in which Edgar Cayce received his information. Repeatedly, science and history have validated concepts and ideas explored in Cayce's psychic information. The wealth of these insights has resulted in hundreds of books that explore various aspects of this man's life and work, not to mention foreign translations around the globe.

As fascinating as the breadth of the material and its accuracy is the activity level of Cayce's mind while he was in the reading state. It was not unusual for Edgar Cayce to be giving a reading, laying on his couch, somehow mentally in touch with another individual and his or her surroundings, activities, and relationships, providing answers to any question imaginable or any time-frame in history, and at the same time have his own personal dream that he could recall upon awakening. Occasionally, it was found that at the same time all this was going on, if an individual in the room with Cayce thought of something, he could respond to their query without even being asked! Even a casual perusal of the Cayce information makes it quite evident that the capacity of this man's mind was not limited to what we might call the conventional parameters of time and space.

Perhaps we can gain insights into this amazing talent from one of Edgar Cayce's own dreams. In 1932, while giving a reading to another individual, Cayce had a dream in which he saw himself as a tiny dot that began to be elevated as if in a whirlwind. As the dot rose, the rings of the whirlwind became larger and larger, each one encompassing a greater span of space than the one which had gone before. There were also spaces between each ring which the sleeping Cayce recognized as the various levels of consciousness development. A reading was given (294-131) confirming that this experience had provided a visual representation of the very thing which transpired as Cayce entered the trance state. The information went on to say, "As indicated, the entity is—in the affairs of the world—a tiny speck, as it were, a mere grain of sand; yet when raised in the atmosphere or realm of the spiritual forces it becomes all inclusive . . . " In other words, as he entered the readings state, he was no longer limited to the confines of space/ time and could make available to himself greater and greater levels of consciousness. It was a talent which would enable him to access insights into virtually anything imaginable.

Once this ability was underway, Edgar Cayce stated that his information was derived from essentially two sources: 1) the subconscious mind of the individual for whom he was giving the reading; and, 2) an etheric source of information, called the "akashic records," which is apparently some kind of universal database for every thought, word, or deed that has ever transpired in the earth. In the language of the readings, these sources are further described as follows:

(Q) *From what source does this body Edgar Cayce derive its information?*

(A) The information as given or obtained from this body is gathered from the sources from which the suggestion may derive its information. In this state the conscious mind becomes subjugated to the subconscious, superconscious or soul mind; and may and does communicate with like minds, and the subconscious or soul force becomes universal. From any subconscious mind information may be obtained, either from this plane or from the impressions as left by the individuals that have gone on before, as we see a mirror reflecting direct that which is before it . . . Through the forces of the soul, through the mind of others as presented, or that have gone on before; through the subjugation of the physical forces in this manner, the body obtains the information. (3744-3)

and,

In giving an interpretation of the records as we find them, it is well—especially for this entity—that there be given a premise from which the reasoning is drawn. Upon time and space is written the thoughts, the deeds, the activities of an entity—as in relationships to its environs, its hereditary influence; as directed—or judgment drawn by or according to what the entity's ideal is. Hence, as it has been oft called, the record is God's book of remembrance; and each entity, each soul—as the activities of a single day of an entity in the material world—either makes same good or bad or indifferent, depending upon the entity's application of self towards that which is the ideal manner for the use of time, opportunity and the *expression* of that for which each soul enters a material manifestation. The interpretation then as drawn here is with the desire and hope that, in opening this for the entity, the experience may be one of helpfulness and hopefulness. (1650-1)

The ability to gather information in this manner may sound unusual, but even today much of the workings of the human mind remain a mystery. Some contemporary research has estimated that the brain filters out as much as ninety-nine percent of the information available to it *(Brain-Mind Bulletin)*. Although this may seem high, how often do we become aware of the sounds made by our heating and air conditioning systems, our own breath, or the car driving next to us in traffic? How frequently are we cognizant of the seat upon which we are sitting, or the weight of our glasses upon our nose? Do we generally let ourselves notice the intensity of colors around us, or even the slight variation in smells within the rooms of our own home? How many times have we driven to a location and then not recalled any portion of the trip that actually got us there? All this information resides just beyond the bounds of conscious awareness and, yet, we are not cognizant of it. Without our brain filters, we probably could not survive all the stresses, distractions, and stimuli that are simply a part of everyday life. Perhaps one component of Cayce's psychic talent was an ability to set aside the very filters which prevent our own sensory system from being overloaded. ESP is simply an extended sense perception. With this in mind, perhaps as amazing as Cayce's extraordinary psychic ability is the fact that he was somehow able to survive and live some semblance of normalcy even while being exposed to such a vast array of incoming data.

This book has been compiled in an attempt to provide the reader with an overview of the types of ESP evidenced in the Edgar Cayce readings.

Although not intended as an encyclopedia of every "psychic happening" in the Cayce files, it does present an amazing variety of case histories and documented stories. Even those previously unsure of the validity of psychic information will have to admit that the story of this man's life and work demands further inquiry. Perhaps it was for this very reason that Edgar Cayce himself never challenged the skeptic, preferring instead to simply extend them an invitation to "come and see."

Chapter 1

# CATEGORIES OF PSYCHIC EXPERIENCE

Today, most individuals are familiar with ESP, Extra Sensory Perception, as the ability to communicate or to receive information without the aid of one of the five senses (taste, smell, hearing, touch, and sight.) Rather than simply combining all psychic experiences into the same category, this extended ability to perceive can also be further broken down and classified. Those categories most frequently demonstrated within Cayce's readings include telepathy, clairvoyance, precognition, and retrocognition.

Telepathy is also known as mind-to-mind communication. This is the ability to obtain information psychically by reading the mind of another person. In our own lives, when we suddenly start thinking about someone we have not heard from, and a short while later the phone rings and that other person is on the line, this is one example of telepathy.

Once, while giving a physical reading for an individual (531-1), Edgar Cayce gave several sentences and a series of words. Meanwhile, his stenographer, Gladys Davis, sitting across the room, was wondering how some of this information should be punctuated. As if in response to her unspoken query, the unconscious Cayce told her to put a comma between the words "body-soul-entity." He went on to describe where a new paragraph should begin as well as where she need to place a set of parentheses. All this was evidence of telepathy because Gladys had simply thought of a question and it was answered without being asked.

A second category of ESP is clairvoyance. Clairvoyance literally means "clear-seeing," but it can also be used to suggest the ability to obtain information, sensations, sounds, even smells through other than the physical senses. When a person perceives information in this manner, it does not necessarily come from another individual. For example, suppose you shuffled a deck of cards and placed them face down, and then went through the deck and tried to name each one. If your percentage of correct guesses went far beyond what could be expected by random chance, it would be an example of clairvoyance. On the other hand, if you tried the same experiment with a friend who carefully looked at each card and concentrated on it before you guessed, this would be an example of telepathy. Although this example is pretty straight-forward, within some case histories of the Cayce files it is difficult to determine whether telepathy or clairvoyance is most in operation.

Repeatedly, the Cayce readings demonstrated documented accounts of clairvoyance. Perhaps two of the most unique cases are readings # 373-1 and 4591-1. In both cases, Cayce was able to speak in foreign languages of which he had no conscious knowledge. In the one case (373), given to a fifty-three-year-old man who had been born in Germany, Cayce merely spoke a couple of German sentences. However, in the other (4591-1) Cayce gave the entire reading in Italian! A local Italian vendor was quickly procured to take down the information in English. The request for the reading had been sent by a gentleman from Palermo, Sicily.

Clairvoyance may also have been demonstrated in an early reading given in 1907 (740-1). An individual who was a practicing lawyer in New York wished to have evidence of Cayce's talent by being psychically "tracked" during the course of one day—at the time, Edgar Cayce was living in Kentucky.

As soon as Cayce began the reading he mentioned the time difference between the two cities—evidently, this was the first occasion he realized that Bowling Green, Kentucky, and New York, New York, were not in the same time zone. During the course of the reading, Cayce described the man's activities. He "saw" the man enter a cigar store. While inside, the man smoked a cigarette and bought a certain brand of cigars. Afterwards, the man went up the street to his office and instead of waiting for the elevator (the reading said, "We will have him walk up so he will remember it") he walked up the steps and Cayce "heard" him whistling a certain song (*Annie Laurie*). In his office, the lawyer found a man waiting for him whose business was regarding a certain piece of property at the end of Williams Street bridge. He turned to his desk and found three letters: a bill, a business letter, and a note from his sweetheart. Cayce then mentioned that the man had a meeting with a man named "Dolligan." This information was all wired by telegram to Mr. [740] in New York. After a number of days, a letter was received in reply:

*Your "reading" as to myself was correct in the*

3

*main. As a matter of fact at the first hour named in your reading I was engaged in preparing papers in a matter for a client residing in Brooklyn. It had to do with an estate of a deceased person, all of which matters are transacted in the Surrogates Court situation situated in the New Hall of Records, which is only a short step from the Brooklyn Bridge connecting New York City and Brooklyn. I did have an engagement for this afternoon to go over a matter with Mr. Downey (not Dolligan), your telegram reaching me two or three hours before that conference was to take place.*

> December 16, 1907
> #740, Attorney and Counsellor at Law
> 52 William Street
> New York

Precognition—the ability to see into the future—is a third category of ESP evidenced within the readings. To a New York businessman interested in investments in the 1920's (case 257-36), Cayce advised the purchase of securities in the communications' industries, stating that radio, and then telephone communications, would one day encircle the globe. In March 1929, six months before the stock market crash, reading 900-425, provided a New York stock broker with a severe warning of the impending "great disturbance in financial circles." For many children, Cayce foresaw what they would be like as adults, even going so far as to describe hidden talents and occupational decisions. In 1941, eight months before the United States had even entered World War II, the readings predicted the arrival of peace in "'45 and '46." (270-47)

Precognition may have been evident in a reading given on January 18, 1925. At the time of the reading, Edgar Cayce lived in Dayton but was on a business trip in New York. He had just completed giving a reading for another case [4599-1] when he began talking about a woman Mrs. [5700] in Eugene, Missouri, who needed assistance. No one in the room knew why the information was being given, but it was written down by the stenographer. The reading said, in part:

[5700]—Missouri. Now, in this condition that has arisen in the body from the dis-arrangement in the pelvic organs, especially those in the false pelvis, we find these need attention at once, through that condition as given, for the operation on the body, else there will be in 19 days the setting up of an infection that will bring destructive forces to the whole system. The alleviation of the pressure has been effective to the body, but this attempt to lift that heavier than the body should have attempted, under the existing conditions, has brought about this condition, or falling more of the organs in the pelvis, and the rupture of the left Fallopian Tube, and these conditions should be attended to at once. (5700-6)

Amazingly, when the Cayce family returned to Dayton several days later, they found a letter from the Missouri woman asking for assistance. Even without knowing about her request for information, all of her questions had been answered in the voluntary reading. In addition to the fact that Cayce did not receive the request for help until he had returned home, it was later determined that [5700's] letter may have even been written *after* the reading was given!

The Cayce files are literally filled with thousands of examples of retrocognition, which is a fourth major category of ESP. In simplest terms, retrocognition is the ability to see into the past. This enabled the readings to zero in on childhood experiences or trauma, the root cause of an illness or a fear, even ancient civilizations and past lives. Although much of the retrocognitive information may be impossible to verify—especially that which deals with the ancient past—repeatedly, Cayce has provided insights into history that have later proven accurate. For example, more than eleven years before the Dead Sea Scrolls were found in 1947, Edgar Cayce provided a great deal of information on a Jewish sect called the Essenes. Cayce claimed that in the Essene society men and women lived and worked together. Scholars, however, believed that the Essenes were a monastic society composed exclusively of men. It was not until archaeological excavations occurred after Cayce's death that the psychic information was verified.

Some of the retrocognitive material deals with the much more recent past and is therefore easier to validate. For example, in reading 1462-1, Edgar Cayce correctly gave the birth place and date of a young woman for whom he was giving a reading, even though he had been mistakenly provided with the incorrect city and date of birth. On a number of occasions when individuals were seeking dream interpretation readings, such as 900-69, Cayce reminded the dreamer of forgotten portions of his or her own dream!

In one of the most celebrated cases of Cayce's early career, retrocognition pinpointed the mental dysfunction and physical convulsions of a six year old girl (case 2473-1) to a fall and an illness she had experienced at the age of two. The girl, Aime Dietrich, had been to specialists for years but no treatment proved effective. Her father's affidavit from October, 1910, states in part: "She was now six years old and getting worse, had as many as twenty convulsions in one day, her mind was a blank, all reasoning power was entirely gone." The reading provided a last chance course of treatment which was followed. The father's affidavit continues:

> ... *he went into a sleep or trance and diagnosed her case as one of congestion at base of the brain, stating also minor details. He outlined to Dr. A.C. Layne [Al C. Layne, D.O.], now of Griffin, Georgia, how to proceed to cure her. Dr. Layne treated her accordingly, every day for three weeks, using Mr. Cayce occasionally to follow up the treatment, as results developed. Her mind began to clear up about the eighth day and within three months she was in perfect health, and is so to this day. This case can be verified by many of the best citizens of Hopkinsville, Kentucky* ...
>
> Signed—C.H. Dietrich

Later, Aime graduated with honors from the University of Kentucky. Unfortunately, as the years passed, the Dietrich and Cayce families moved and were no longer in touch with one another. Aime contracted tuberculosis and died in 1934 at the age of thirty-seven.

Whether it's telepathy, clairvoyance, precognition, or retrocognition, the Edgar Cayce material provides an impressive collection of documented case histories for further investigation, research, and inquiry. In fact, what may be most unique about the more than 14,000 readings given by Edgar Cayce over a period of forty-three years is the attending documentation. More than simply the readings themselves, every stenographic transcript includes the names of all individuals present, the location, time, date, and other pertinent information. In addition to background reports explaining why the individual was asking specific information or how he or she found out about Mr. Cayce, there are accompanying reports, letters, and follow-up corroboration. This meticulous attention to detail makes it possible to state with complete certainty that Edgar Cayce remains the most carefully witnessed, investigated and documented psychic of all time.

# Chapter 2

# TELEPATHY AND CLAIRVOYANCE

Edgar Cayce's uncanny psychic ability was proceeded by putting himself into a self-induced trance. For each reading, he would lie down on a couch, become comfortable, put his hands up to his forehead, and begin to pray. When he saw a brilliant flash of light, it was the signal that he could continue. He would lower his hands to his stomach, and when his eyelids began to flutter, the conductor (most often his wife) would give him the appropriate suggestion. In this state, it seemed that he could answer any question or provide any type of information requested.

Oftentimes, he would begin speaking as though he could see specific details of what was occurring around an individual at that very moment in time—even though the person might be hundreds of miles away. Throughout this chapter are examples of telepathy and clairvoyance as discussed in the introduction.

Examples of such ability, and subsequent reports, are as follows:

*Case #5196-1*

Gertrude Cayce: You will go over this body carefully, examine it thoroughly and tell me the conditions you find at the present time, giving the cause of the existing conditions, also suggestions for help and relief of this body; answering the questions as I ask them.

Edgar Cayce: Yes, not bad-looking pajamas! We have the body here [subject in California]. As we find, there are disturbing conditions. There has been in the body, for some time back, conditions wherein the tautness in the bronchi and trachea, with the taxation of the muscular and nerve forces, has produced weaknesses and allergies.

Report: Mr. [5196]'s letter: *In answer to your letter inquiring for a report on the Physical Reading given for me . . . Yes, I deliberately donned a pair of new pajamas of a bright color. The diagnosis was the same as several chiropractors had given me before and several after.*

*Case #549-1*

Edgar Cayce: Yes, we have the body here, [549], Millinery Department [in Tennessee] . . . now waiting on a lady in front of a glass with knot on posts—two sit together, you see—on the back one. Yes, quite an interesting lady, though, she is waiting on; she needs a reading, too! to take this knot off of her! As we find with this body, [549], there are those conditions that disturb the better physical functioning of the body. These, as we find, affect the digestive system as well as the general circulation, and are of the natures that affect the tissue in portions of the body; especially in the lower pelvic organs, making reflex conditions through the nerve systems.

Report: Miss [243]'s letter: *Mrs. [542] and Miss [549] are both so happy with their readings ... they are both taking treatments from the same osteopath, Dr. Watson—a woman, and they say she was delighted with the diagnosis and is treating by the reading. Miss [549]'s was funny, wasn't it, when it started off? She is a designer and said she was helping Mrs. Miller with a hat. She said she thought Mrs. Miller would get a reading.*

Miss [549]'s letter: *The reading is splendid and I wish to say I do feel greatly relieved. I am taking the osteopathic treatment, at present I have had five treatments ... I do really feel much better, altho I still have a little aching in the lower part of my body.*

*Case #1100-27*
Hugh Lynn Cayce: You will give the physical condition of this body at the present time [located in Pennsylvania], with suggestions for further corrective measures; answering the questions she submits, as I ask them:

Edgar Cayce: [When locating the street and number]—That's a right pretty tree on the corner! Yes; we have the body here, [1100]; this we have had before. As we find, the general physical forces of the body are very good—in the present.

Report: Mrs. [1100]'s letter: *Thank you so much for the readings and your dear letter. Yes, there is an unusually lovely tree on the corner of our apartment building. The building is four stories high and the tree is slightly taller.*

Case #1100-14
[Physical suggestion given]
Edgar Cayce: Yes—982 [repeating address]—
That's a very nice place! [Subject in Florida.]
We have the body, [1100]; this we have had
before. Improvements are still indicated in
the body, and as we find if there are the pre-
cautions taken, not too soon beginning to
overtax the body, the body should continue
to be on the improve.

Report: [1100]'s letter: *The reading came yes-
terday and I want to thank you very much. I
was quite amused when the information
said, "A very nice place," because it is just that
and the people here are lovely . . . Clearwater
is very small but quite pretty and this hotel is
unusually nice. Lounge rooms and sun porches
galore, also a beautiful roof on which I can
take sun baths after I get stronger. Am trying
to take it slowly, as I know too much sun is
very bad, especially when one still runs a bit
of temperature. Know that will be leaving me
shortly . . . Am trying very hard to "work at
the play and play at the work of getting well."
Thank you so much.*

Case #3904-1
[Physical suggestion given]
Edgar Cayce: 1075 Park Avenue, Apt. . . . very
unusual in some of these halls, isn't it—what
funny paintings! Yes—we have the body
here, [3904].

Report from [3904]: *Dr. found spinal condition to exist, just as described by Mr. Cayce.
Treated accordingly several months . . . Oste-
opathy, with special attention to 3rd and 4th
lumbar centers . . . [regarding the "funny*

*paintings"] Yes—include wood plaques from Central America and other unusual wall adornments.*

*Case #930-1*
Gertrude Cayce: You will have before you the body and enquiring mind of [930], located at . . . 34th Street [subject in New York], who seeks information, advice and guidance as to his mental and material welfare. You will answer the questions he has submitted, as I ask them.

Edgar Cayce: Yes (he's on his way), we have the enquiring mind, [930] . . .

Report: Letter from [257]: . . . *It was very wonderful on the reading for [930]—that he was on the bus at 3:20 and was late at Dr. [ . . . ] office—but you said he was enroute and he was. He requires a lot of help . . . You will be able to help him also in his decision of the new position . . .*

Letter from [930]: . . . *At the appointed time of the reading I was unfortunately delayed, while enroute started to concentrate, offered up my prayer to the Almighty to give me guidance thru you.*

Edgar Cayce's psychic prowess with telepathy, or mind-to-mind communication, is certainly evident in each of these cases, but most often the information received in his readings goes far beyond simple "mind reading." In thousands of cases, with no information other than a name and address, Edgar Cayce described exact symptoms, named specific ailments, and then outlined detailed regimens of treatment.

On November 12, 1943, an interesting reading presented itself. Edgar Cayce had nearly finished giving three readings for people who had written to him for help (3368, 3498, and 2390). Unbeknown to Cayce's wife, Gertrude, who was conducting the readings, or his stenographer, Gladys, who was taking down the information, in another part of the house a member of the office staff was speaking on the phone to a woman in Charlottesville, Virginia, who was extremely upset. Her daughter (308), who had received readings from Cayce in the past, had fallen out of a bunk bed at college and possibly injured her spine. Unable to walk, the girl had been confined to the infirmary at the College of William and Mary in Williamsburg, Virginia.

When the three assigned readings for the day were completed, rather than waking up, the sleeping Cayce continued speaking and volunteered the following information:

Now we have those conditions that exist with . . . [in an undertone] Charlottesville— Williamsburg. These are bruises, though the structural portions also are bruised. Apply Glyco-Thymoline packs in those areas, as on hips and the spine, as well as in the 3rd cervical center. Then apply heat, not with an electric pad but with heavy salt heated in pads or bags. This will remove the strain as well as alkalize the drainages that must necessarily be set up by the use at this particular time of a senna base laxative, such as Dr. Caldwell's Syrup of Pepsin. This would be good for the body. Keep the Glyco-Thymoline packs. Change them about every three to four hours. Keep them on for about the same length of time and then leave off, but next day use them again—until this soreness disappears. After tomorrow, begin to set up drainages by massage . . . Yes, this is

14

the twelfth—we haven't made a mistake! We are through. (308-12)

Neither Gladys nor Gertrude understood why the information had been given, but it was taken down nonetheless. Later that same day, the incident was discussed with the member of the office staff who had been on the phone. Suddenly everything made sense. A follow-up report from the girl's mother states:

*My daughter, [308], was trying to get in bed—the top side of a double decker, at William & Mary College. She slipped on the chair and hit the end of her spine. By the next morning she couldn't get out of bed and was taken to the infirmary. Her room mate called me about 10 A.M., on 11/12/43. I then received a call from the doctor at the infirmary and he wanted to know if I wanted some x-rays made; I told him I would let him know. Then I phoned Mr. Cayce's home and talked with Harmon Bro [a member of the office staff], who explained that so many readings were scheduled that he didn't think [308]'s could be gotten in today—it was too late to mention it to Mr. Cayce since he had already started the check physical readings for the morning, but he would tell him later. I was so confused that I prayed constantly for guidance. At 9 P.M. that night I phoned Gladys and asked her how long she thought it would be before a check reading could be gotten. She said, "We got it—it came through at the end of the other readings, without the suggestion being given to obtain it!" . . . Evidently my anxiety in Charlottesville had gotten through to him . . . We followed the treatments for three days and she returned to school. She has never had any trouble since.*

The files within the vault of the Edgar Cayce Foundation are filled with testimonials and follow-up confirmations, not only by the patients themselves but also by doctors and other medical authorities. All of this information is open to the public and available for personal research and investigation. These testimonies, reports, even X-ray corroboration, provide subsequent confirmation of Cayce's diagnosis as well as the effectiveness of his prescribed treatments.

In case 551-1, a reading was requested by a young man in New York City who made no comment about his condition. Later, after the reading, a doctor confirmed the information provided from the trance state. A portion of the reading and attending documentation are as follows:

> Edgar Cayce: . . . These conditions, as we find, have to do with certain centers in the nerve system that are impinged in such manner as to prevent the circulation, especially in the eliminating and incentive receiving centers, causing an unequalized amount of dross or refuse to accumulate in various portions of the body, forming self then in to that mass or condition in tissue and fibre of the system known as catarrhal conditions, such as exist in the inner ear, nose, intestines, in stomach proper. These all then, at various times, show the excess of this condition forming in the system. The radiations from these centers, then, which are depressed, as we find come from the 12th, 11th, 10th dorsal and in the 5th and 4th cervicals. These affect then the circulation as directed from these portions and prevent the tissue receiving the incentive to produce

perfect eliminations in the system. We have this excess created, as we find, after there has been especial nerve tension, or an excess of foods with the body under nerve tension. The body becomes easily irritated under such conditions, having what would be termed blue or gloomy days, to which the mind, the whole system, seems to submerge at such times. These, then, are symptoms. These, then, are the conditions in physical to which the body should be warned, or from which take warning.

To remove those conditions, and to bring the body where the physical may function normally and nominally, would be to first have these subluxations removed by manipulation, osteopathically preferably given, in these regions as given, and so stimulate by heat (any vibration may be used; Alpine Ray, Violet ray, Radial ray. Any that stimulate nerve and blood secretion through parts that have been subluxated), and with this stimulus we will find the body would respond readily through physical forces. These, then, would be necessary three to five treatments, taken one every other day, until the system is in its normal position, condition. Then it will be necessary only to take them once a month, or such a matter, or when necessary for the body to gain its physical, mental, equilibrium.

Report: letter from Mr. [551]: *This is in reference to your reading of the 12th [and] instructions concerning my health and business success. Following your instructions I have placed myself under the care of an able osteopath, Dr. Joseph Ferguson . . . who has found by his examinations your reading cor-*

*rect in every detail, except a few minor defects
which are now being treated in conjunction
with your given suggestions. This afternoon
was my fifth treatment...*

Letter from attending physician: *Dear Mr.
Cayce: I take pleasure in reporting to you regarding the case of Mr. [551] who consulted
me on March 17th, following your report to
him on his physical condition. I found the
cervical and lower dorsal subluxations which
you mentioned and also the third, fourth and
fifth dorsals were somewhat anterior. Mr.
[551] is having these mechanical conditions
corrected and they have already shown considerable improvement. I am raying him
with the Ultra-Violet Ray by means of the Alpine Lamp, which is the name given to the
air cooled, mercury quartz lamp made by
The Hanovia Chemical Co., of Newark, N.J. ...
Mr. [551] is resting much better and shows
considerable improvement in every way.*

*Yours respectfully,*
Joseph Ferguson, D.O.
Osteopathic Society
of the City of New York

In another instance [case 556-5], a Norfolk
man was taken violently ill one June evening.
Neither his wife, himself, or their physician could
figure out what was wrong until after Cayce's diagnosis. His wife later reported:

*He went for a walk . . . and was brought
home by a friend. He was suffering severe
pain in the head, and vomited quantities of
blood. The next day, I called an osteopath
and a physician to try to determine the cause
of the condition. The physician believed it
was either a sinus or perhaps an abscessed*

*tooth, and advised [him to consult] his dentist. I phoned our dentist [who] came, and stated the condition was not from his teeth. By this time, he was suffering excruciating pain, and his head and face were swelling. The dentist advised my calling a specialist. My husband protested against such a procedure, and begged me to allow no one to touch his head or mouth.*

*I sat a moment in deliberation, and...it was then, Mr. Cayce came to my mind. I called on the phone, and Miss Gladys answered. I said, "Mr. [556] is seriously ill; ask Mr. Cayce if he will give a reading. I want to know one thing: Where is the source of infection?" I gave no description of his condition, nor any of the symptoms . . . the doctors did not know what was causing the illness.*

An emergency reading was requested. While the man remained in Norfolk, across town, twenty miles away in Virginia Beach, Edgar Cayce was able to describe the problem, " . . . there is a closing—as it were—in the area of the emptying of the stomach in the duodenum. And this causes those portions where these is some bloating or swelling; great pains through the abdominal area, through even the face and those portions where the connections are with same. " The wife's report continues:

*Lengthy details were given as to course of treatment, all of which I followed to the letter, calling for additional advice from time to time, and following each of them closely. He had lost weight very fast, and by October had gained back all of it. By November he was restored to normal health. Words fail me to express to you, and to the world, the wonderful merits of the information that comes through the readings. Scientifically speaking, a condition of this kind is seldom overcome without an operation, and then taking a patient from 12 to 18 months to recover therefrom.*

A questionnaire completed by the family physician contained the following report:

(1) Did the reading presented to you describe the condition of the patient?
(A) *Yes. I confirmed it with the "Pathodast Blood Testing" instrument.*
(2) Were the suggestions for your treatment in your opinion proper for this condition?
(A) *Yes.*
(3) For what period of time has the patient followed directions given in the reading under your care?
(A) *The full time.*
(4) What results have you observed?
(A) *Excellent.*
(5) Comment.
(A) *The specific infections [were] streptococci, colisepsis, acidosis and general anemia.*
Signed—Dr. Carl S. Frischkorn

Not unexpectedly, oftentimes, the doctor to whom the patient went in order to follow the treatments outlined in the readings insisted on obtaining his or her own diagnosis. In the case of 565-1, the woman had been in extremely poor health for approximately eight or nine years. Her symptoms included pains in the top of the head, dizziness, lack of appetite, excess kidney activity, etc. Mrs. [565] took her reading to a new physician who refused to follow the advice until he had made his own diagnosis and checked her X-rays. As a means of demonstrating the thoroughness of Cayce's clairvoyant insights, a majority of the reading she received follows:

Text of reading 565-1
May 30, 1934
[Cayce in Virginia, patient in North Carolina]

Edgar Cayce: Yes, we have the body here, [565].

Now, as we find, while there are many conditions physical with this body that are very good, there are those conditions that with the correction would make a much better body physically and mentally for the activities in the mental, spiritual and material body.

The disturbances, as we find, have to do with some minor conditions respecting functionings of organs, and little or no organic disorder. While many portions of the system are involved at one time or another, the conditions are such that they may be easily corrected in the present.

These, then, are conditions as we find them with this body, [565]:

First, in the *blood supply*, here we find the form of an anemia, or the lack of a proper balance in the numbers of the red blood cells and the white blood cells. This condition, while of an active nature, *changes* at times; for we may find at times there would be almost sufficient in numbers of the red and quite a deficiency in the white, while again we may find an alteration in just the opposite direction. This arises from nervous conditions that disturb the circulation, and

21

the assimilation of that taken as food values for the body. The nerve disturbance arises, as we shall see, from two—yea, three—distinct causes, making a combination of disorders contributory—as will be seen—one to another. Hence there is not only the variation in the red and white blood supply, or the form of anemia, but the character of the disturbance in other portions of the body, as we shall see.

As to the characterization of the blood itself; that is, the hemoglobin, the urea, the activity in its coagulation and in the blood count; this varies, not so much as to cause what may be termed an unbalanced metabolism but the very character of the nervous condition makes low blood pressure and at times disturbances to the heart's activity and its pulsation. Dizziness arises at times from distinct causes, during the periods of the menstrual activity in elimination and during the periods when there is overexhaustion by excitement to the nerve forces of the body, or at other times we may find it arising purely from gases that form from nervous indigestion. These changes and alterations in the pressure cause changes in the character of the blood itself, though the body may not be said to have a blood disturbance—but the functioning of the organs themselves and their activity upon the system through the nerve supply makes the disturbance, though the character of the blood so far as carrying poisons or any character of bacilli in same is lacking; for it is very good in these directions.

In the *nerve forces* of the body we find much that is a cause, and much that is an effect. So, it is not altogether nerves; though the body is nervous naturally from those conditions that have existed and do exist in the body, but under stress or strain no one would call the body, [565], a nervous person; for she would be very quiet and very determined and very set in what she would do, and she would do it!

In the cerebrospinal system we find there has been a relaxation in the 3rd and 4th dorsal area that has tended to make for a relaxing in the *position* of the stomach itself, or the organs or the nerve tendons and muscular forces through the hypogastric and pneumogastric plexus, as to allow the stomach itself to tilt to the lower side, or the pyloric end up and the hypogastric or the cardiac and lower than normal, you see. This makes for a tendency of easy fermentation in same, and is a natural strain on the nerve system. The muscular reactions cause the condition, but the effect is in the nerve system; and as those plexus in the upper dorsal are in close connection or association with the sympathetic and sensory nerve reactions through the ganglia near the 1st, 2nd and 3rd dorsal area, this makes for a slowing of the circulation to the head, you see, sympathetically. Hence organs of the sensory system *sympathetically* become involved, as at times there is the tendency for a quick drying of the throat—and the body feels like it would spit cotton often! At other times we have a thumping or drumming in the ear. At others there are the tendencies for the conditions to produce irritations and burnings in the eyes, especially if there has been an eyestrain either by being in the wind, poor light or strong light; any of these will produce an irritation through the necessary energies used and the lack of supply of nerve energy from the depletion in the area as indicated.

From this sympathetic condition, both as to the nerve supplies to the organs of digestion and as to the activities in the eliminations of the body during the periods that should be natural or normal, the reactions also produce an irritation again which causes the secretions from the vagina in such measures or manners as to make irritations so that the body is irritable in manner; and until the flow has begun there are pains produced in top of head, dizziness, lack of appetite, and an excess activity of the kidneys or bladder. These are purely reflex and are sympathetic conditions, as we have indicated, from a subluxation in the 3rd and 4th dorsal plexus area.

As to the activities of the *organs* themselves:

In the brain forces the reactions and activities are near normal.

The organs of the sensory system, as indicated, are disturbed through reflex conditions arising from the upper dorsal and reflexly through the cervical area.

Lungs, bronchi, larynx, only at periods when there are irritations to the hypogastric area is there any disorder of a nature not normal, but this will be corrected when the corrections are made throughout the system.

The digestive system, as indicated, shows disturbances; not only as to position of the stomach itself but as related to the digestive activities and reflexly to the heart's activity through poor circulation impoverished by the inactivity of that assimilated being prop-

erly directed in the system, and sympathetically also for the organs of the pelvis in their
activity.

The liver, spleen, pancreas, as we find,
would function near normal when there is a
normalcy from the position or the activities
of the body. When there are those changes
that may be brought about by the addition
of those properties necessary for creating a
balance in the system, these will make for
proper activity throughout the body.

Then, in making the corrections for this
body, [565], we are speaking of:

First we would begin with making the
proper adjustments osteopathically, especially—or specifically—in the upper dorsal
area, *coordinating* the rest of the ganglia and
the activity of the organs with same as these
corrections are made. As we find, this would
not require more than sixteen such adjustments and treatments.

Begin immediately, when the body rests,
with having the feet very much higher than
the head; and after such a rest there should
be the holding of the stomach better in position by the use of bandage or belt about
the body. Not so tight as to cause discom-
fort, but as the manipulations and adjustments are made let these be of *sufficient*
activity as to *hold* the position of the stomach, that the activities through same may be
kept in their proper relationship with the
rest of the system.

For those disturbances that have been
produced by the nerve reaction to the other
organs of the system, so as to make that in-
centive for the corrections being made to
coordinate with the activities of the glands
and functioning of the organs, we would

take a compound put together in this manner; adding the ingredients in the order named:

To 16 ounces of distilled water, we would add; stirring in; beating fine or powdering each ingredient: Dried Wild Ginseng Root (rolled together or beat very fine), 1 ounce; Indian Turnip, 1/2 dram; Wild Ginger (now this isn't Wild Ginseng, but Ginger—which is a different root entirely), 1 dram. Boil slowly until it will amount to, when strained, 12 ounces. Then add to the solution 2 ounces pure grain alcohol and 1 ounce Syrup or Essence of Wild Cherry. See? The dose would be 1/2 teaspoonful twice each day, morning on arising before the meal and when ready to retire. And continue taking until the whole quantity has been taken, you see.

Keep the manipulations about twice each week, making corrections specifically in the upper dorsal area and the *general* conditions throughout the body made to coordinate with same.

This would be an outline for the diet, though it may be altered as the seasons change, you see:

Mornings—citrus fruit or dry cereals with fruit or berries and milk, but do not use the citrus fruits and the cereals at the same meal, or quantities of milk with the citrus fruit. Very crisp bacon with browned bread, coddled egg or the like may be taken at the same meal. These may be altered at times to fresh fruits or stewed fruits, stewed rhubarb or the like, which are well but change them from time to time.

Noons—either a liquid diet or a green fresh-vegetable diet; such as juices of vegetables, juices of meats, but do not combine the green vegetables and the soups—or the liquid diet *with* the green or fresh vegetables. Include all the vegetables that may be eaten in a salad. And if there is to be taken any pastry, pie, cake, cream or the like, eat it at the noon meal—not in the evening or morning meals.

Evenings—preferably well-cooked vegetables, with at least one period each day (either morning or evening—and well that it be altered) of beef *juices;* not the meats but the beef juices made fresh every few days, not large quantities, but that we may change the activities in the system as to the correction in the blood supply. The meats should be rather those of fowl, liver, tripe, pigs' feet, or the like. Any of these should be included as to meats, but the greater portion should be of vegetables—with meats such as these taken at least three times each week.

Do these and, as we find, in thirty-six to forty days we will have a body quite a bit changed and near normal.

From a distance of more than 150 miles away, Edgar Cayce gave the woman a thorough examination (including X-rays!), discussed symptoms which had not been communicated to him, outlined a regimen of treatment which included physiotherapy, diet, and massage, and—in spite of her years of difficulty—provided reassurance that she could regain her health. Certainly, much more than telepathy is at work here. Mrs. [565] was so thrilled and encouraged by her reading that she told her sister she "wouldn't take $5 million dollars for it." Accompanying reports from the woman and her doctor are as follows:

Report: letter from Mrs. [565]: *When the*

*reading was received I was determined to carry it out to the letter if possible. I went to the Tucker-Carson Sanitarium in Raleigh, and the reading was turned over to Dr. Tucker. I asked him if he would treat me as suggested in the reading. After reading it he said he would not treat me as suggested, and would give me no treatment at all until after he had made a thorough examination, which I submitted to. I went to his office 4 days in succession. I was X-rayed several times and was given a very thorough examination. At the completion of this I was informed that his diagnosis of my case including the X-ray pictures were identical to the diagnosis in the reading, after which he treated me as suggested in the reading. I followed the diet as closely as possible and after several treatments I began to feel some improvements. I continued with the treatment and took every treatment as suggested in the reading. I can truthfully say that I feel better than I have felt in years. I can drive my car and go any place that I wish at any time, something I have not been able to do in years. I am indeed most grateful to you.*

Letter from Dr. Tucker: *Mrs. [565] was under our care for about six weeks, her last treatment being July 31st, 1934. We made Gastrointestinal X-ray and checked her up physically for every angle. Your diagnosis was verified by our physical findings and we followed closely as possible your suggestions as to treatment. Mrs. [565] made splendid progress under treatment and she told me today that she is much better than she has been for a long time. I appreciate your referring Mrs. [565] to us and will be glad to co-operate with you in any case you send. We certainly appre-*

*ciate your recommending the other three pa-
tients you mentioned in your letter, and if
they come to us we will do our very best for
them.*

*Sincerely,*
*Dr. A. R. Tucker*
*Tucker-Carson Sanitarium*
*Raleigh, N.C.*

Nearly two-thirds of the readings deal with matters of health, covering every imaginable illness and disease that existed during Cayce's lifetime. His recommendations for treatment drew from every medical discipline and prescribed all manner of therapies from diet, exercise and physiotherapy, to prescription medication and even surgery. He was not a psychic healer, instead he provided intuitive insights as to the nature of the illness and outlined a series of recommendations for the individual to help them become well. Most of these recommendations needed to be carried out by a medical professional.

Although thousands of cases provided patients with hope and a specific regimen to follow, on occasion, even the readings could not be optimistic. One example is the case of a sixty-nine-year-old man:

*Case #550-10*
(Physical suggestion.)
Edgar Cayce: Yes—quite serious. Little may be offered as changes from those being administered in the present. For, these—unless there is better coordination in the heart's activity—are close to separations [death]. Keep the body quiet.

Later, Edgar Cayce received a newspaper clipping from the family announcing that the man had died the very next day.

On a few occasions, Cayce's psychic diagnosis could not be substantiated. An example is the case of a fifty-eight year old man with stomach ulcers as well as a tumor on his left arm. The reading described how a nervous shock had produced a detrimental reaction throughout the entire nervous system. However, the chief warning seemed in regards to a blood condition. The reading states, in part:

> The blood . . . is in an impoverished condition. There is a lack of the proper constituents to make the perfect distributing within the blood produced by the organic conditions that are found through the digestive track, and the stomach itself. The effect it has had on the circulation is to reduce the vital forces within the body. There is insufficient hemoglobin of the nature that produces sufficient carbon in the blood to take from the system the poisons that are created by the condition in the stomach and intestinal tract . . . (13-1)

After Mr. [13] received his reading, he went to a physician in order to confirm Cayce's diagnosis. The man's letter suggests that the reading was incorrect:

> Report: letter from [13]: . . . *I had my physician make a test of my blood and he says my blood is in fine condition—test 100%. He says my color is extra fine. Do you suppose a mistake was made . . . ?*

Fifteen years later the man died. According to the death certificate, the cause was "Acute Monocytic Leukemia."

In case 3599-1, a woman had asked for a reading and stated that she could be found one and a half miles northeast of a certain highway. In giving the reading, Cayce corrected her and stated: "One and one half miles northeast—yes, it's one and five-eighths."

For a thirty-four-year-old deep sea diver (case 1395-1), the readings described the location of the Lusitania, provided a lengthy description of the ship's structural integrity upon the ocean floor, gave an estimated worth of the gold bullion still locked in the ship's strong room, and discussed the bodies that were still trapped within the wreckage.

To an individual who was getting ready to leave their house in spite of the reading appointment time, Cayce said, "Come back here and sit down!" (3601-1)

"Yes," he stated after locating the individual for whom he was given the reading, "they have had an accident right in front of the house." (599-10)

Whether it was psychic diagnosis or the ability to describe events as they occurred on the other side of a continent, the documentation in the Cayce files makes it apparent that the readings were not bounded by the confines of time and space. Somehow, while in the trance state, Edgar Cayce had access to information not consciously known to any other individual. Whether the information came from the subconscious mind of the person for whom he was giving the reading, or from some type of akashic record, it becomes apparent that his mind could be elevated to an almost universal consciousness. It was an ability that frequently allowed Edgar Cayce an extended sense perception, even into the future.

Chapter 3

# PRECOGNITION

Although Edgar Cayce accurately predicted countless events, he remained insistent that nothing which dealt with the future was fixed or destined. Instead, because of the nature of free will and choice, the future was not unalterably written. For that reason, a number of individuals were given readings which presented distinct possibilities for their lives depending upon how they themselves exercised their own free wills. One of the most striking cases in this regard was given to the parents of an eleven year old boy who were told that their son could become "a Jesse James" or a "Beethoven."

*Case #3633-1*
Edgar Cayce: Yes, we have the records here of that entity now known as or called [3633].

In giving the interpretations of the records here of this entity, it would be very easy to interpret same either in a very optimistic or a very pessimistic vein. For there are great possibilities and great obstacles. But know, in either case, the real lesson is within self.

For here is the opportunity for an entity (while comparisons are odious, these would be good comparisons) to be either a Beethoven or a Whittier or a Jesse James or some such entity! For the entity is inclined to think more highly of himself than he ought to think, as would be indicated. That's what these three individuals did, in themselves. As to the application made of it, depends upon the individual self.

Here is an entity who has abilities and faculties latent within self which may be turned into music or poetry, or writing in prose, which few would ever excel. Or there may be the desire to have its own way to such an extent that the entity will be in the position to disregard others altogether in every form, just so self has its own way . . .

As to the abilities of the entity in the present, that to which it may attain and how:

There are unlimited abilities. How will they be directed by the entity? How well may others cause the entity to be aware of such activities? These should be the questions in self.

Study to know first thy ideals, spiritual, mental and material. Then apply self in such a manner towards those that there will never be a question mark after thine own conscience nor in the eyes even of others.

Remember that the Lord loveth the cheerful giver as well as those who seek His face.

Ready for questions.

*(Q) What should be his chief work?*

(A) This depends upon what he chooses—whether in music, directing music, writing of music, or writing of verse. But in either of these channels, there may be the greater outlet. The voice of the wood, the voice of the air—any of those are the realms through which the entity may exceed, as well as succeed.

*(Q) Should all of his talents be developed?*
(A) All his talents will either be developed, or run to seed and be drained off.

Report: 2/14/44 letter from [3633]'s Mother:
*... Your reading for [3633] was no surprise to my husband and me. We early saw that such tremendous energy should be set to work, and he is in his third year at a very strict, very religious boarding school. Idleness would destroy him. He must always be in the big world where he will be just a "drop in the bucket"— not the "big frog in a small pond" ...*
Report: 9/49 Letter from [3633]'s Mother: ...
*We are in great distress now over the condition of our only child who has a distressing mental and nervous upset which as yet has not been diagnosed ...*
Report: 3/7/51 Letter from [3633]'s Mother:
*... The press has been cruel to us in our sorrow, and no doubt you have read of our tragedy. My son [3633], who has been emotionally unbalanced for 3 years, last Wednesday shot his father and grandmother. Hugh Lynn, your Father was my friend and I brought [3633] to see him and also he gave a life reading for him which had plenty of warnings in it. I am writing to ask you to please get one of your prayer circles to work on us—and to pour spiritual power into my mother [ ... ] and into my husband [...] and my son [3633]. We certainly need it ...*
Report: 4/26/51 letter from [3633]'s Mother:
*... Thanks so much for your letter about my son [3633]. In the light of our tragic happen-*

*ings, your Father's reading for him takes on*
*great significance . . .*
Report: 8/51 letter from [3633]'s Mother: . . .
*We have had some correspondence about my*
*son [3633] and your Father's reading for him*
*in which he foretold much that has come to*
*pass. [3633] is now in . . . State Hospital. The*
*doctors have of course, there and elsewhere*
*in other sanitariums where he has been, la-*
*beled his trouble, dementia praecox, schizo-*
*phrenia, etc. . . . Thank God his intellect seems*
*intact, he writes for books he has always liked*
*and he takes two newspapers.*
Report from file: *[3633] died on 12/31/63.*

Just as is evidenced in the above case, the readings frequently stated that an individual's free
will had an enormous impact upon his or her future. For that reason, precognition was much
more subject to alteration and change whereas
clairvoyance, telepathy, and retrocognition were
not. When Edgar Cayce predicted a future—for
an individual, a nation, or even the world—it was
a future based on currents events and probable
directions. If events continued to move along the
same course—if people's attitudes, activities, and
external conditions remained the same—then
Edgar Cayce could somewhere project this information onto a future time-line and "see" the results. In spite of the many variables affecting
precognition, time and again what the readings
saw came to pass.

In 1935, in an amazing display of precognitive
perception, Edgar Cayce warned a twenty-nine
year old freight agent [416] of catastrophic events
which were building within the international
community. In response to a question regarding
global affairs, the readings described an entire
world at war. Although not seeing the picture as

necessarily an unchangeable destiny, Cayce warned that "tendencies in the hearts and souls of men are such" that these conditions could be brought about:

*Case #416-7*
Edgar Cayce: . . . As to the affairs of an international nature, these we find are in a condition of great anxiety on the part of many; not only as individuals but as to nations.

And the activities that have already begun have assumed such proportions that there is to be the attempt upon the part of groups to penalize, or to make for the associations of groups to carry on same.

This will make for the taking of sides, as it were, by various groups or countries or governments. This will be indicated by the Austrians, Germans, and later the Japanese joining in their influence; unseen, and gradually growing to those affairs where there must become, as it were, almost a direct opposition to that which has been the *theme* of the Nazis (the Aryan). For these will gradually make for a growing of animosities.

And unless there is interference from what may be called by many the *supernatural* forces and influences, that are activative in the affairs of nations and peoples, the whole *world*—as it were—will be set on fire by the militaristic groups and those that are "for" power and expansion in such associations.

An investment banker came to Edgar Cayce with a request for personal guidance as well as any information that might be provided of a "national and international" nature. The date was March 26, 1935, and the individual, Mr. [261], was interested in obtaining counsel regarding the financial stability of investments and the Federal government. He was warned to wait until after April 15 to make any new investments because of some "unexpected activity" that might cause changes on the national scene. Cayce advised the gentleman that if the changes came, "then there *may* be anxiety in all directions for the American public." When asked what kind of changes he was referring to, Cayce replied, "Accidents in officials of higher position." The reading continues:

*Case #261-14*
Edgar Cayce: . . . These associations, then, come from the sojourn of individuals in an environment such that the correlation of activities from many quarters will work with the individual's application of knowledge. Not that this is *destined* irrespective of what may happen! For many have been the calamitous conditions averted, even in this country—especially through the period of February. Again we are approaching same now, in between this and the 5th and 6th day of April, with the leader in this country—or Roosevelt, when there will be adverse conditions . . .

Just as foretold in the information, ten days after the reading was given there was an assassination attempt on the President's life. The AP news service broadcast a story a week later regarding the attempted assassin.

Newspaper Report: *MAN WHO THREATENED ROOSEVELT FOUND INSANE—Boston, April 12—(AP)—Thomas F. Murphy, a 27-year-old unemployed laborer, who was arrested a week ago for threatening President Roosevelt with assassination, was reported*

37

*tonight by U. S. Marshal John J. Murphy to*
*have been found insane after observation at*
*the Boston Psychopathic Hospital.*

Rather than seeing events as fated or predestined, the Edgar Cayce readings described individuals as being instrumental in "co-creating" their lives. However, most frequently this process was overlooked in the rush and hassle of everyday life and people were not taking the time to become aware of events they were actually creating for their tomorrows. As one example, the readings suggested that individuals were forgetting their true spiritual nature. This neglect was setting events in motion which would create turmoils and strife within the country. In June of 1939, while giving a reading on "the American nation, its ideals, principles and purposes," Edgar Cayce predicted the outcome:

> Ye are to have turmoils—ye are to have strifes between capital and labor. Ye are to have a division in thine own land before there is the second of the Presidents that next will not live through his office—a mob rule! (3976-24)

This reading may have foretold the death of Franklin Roosevelt, the assassination of John F. Kennedy, and the race rights of the 1960s. Again, rather than being preordained, in this same reading Cayce had advised the nation to "give God a chance." By so doing, individuals would begin to remember their spiritual nature and there would be no racial or social problems within the U.S. Instead, there would be "more of patience, more tolerance, more thought of others . . . "

Rather than requesting information on the nation or the world as a whole, most frequently, individuals were interested in events that affected them closer to home—in their personal lives and in their communities. The Cayce files are filled with predictions of this nature. For example, in July of 1932, a land developer from the Norfolk/Virginia Beach area was interested in the potential growth of the city and its surroundings. A portion of the reading and the case file reports are as follows:

*Case #5541-2*
Edgar Cayce: . . . With the years that are to come, conditions that are to arise, as we find, eventually—and this within the next thirty years—Norfolk, with its environs, is to be the chief port on the East coast, this not excepting Philadelphia or New York; the second being rather in the New England area . . . .

*(Q) What is the future of Virginia Beach?*
(A) This, as we find, would require a great deal of speculation on the part of individuals. As *we* would find, and as we would give, of all the resorts that are in the East coast, Virginia Beach will be the first and the longest lasting of the increasing of the population, valuation, and activities. Hence, as we would give, the future is *good.*

Report from *Virginian-Pilot,* Sunday, 3/15/70: *BEACH GOES BOOM . . . The history of Virginia Beach as a town actually began . . . [with] the construction of a clubhouse for hunting and fishing in 1880 . . . A few summer cottages were built along the oceanfront and the occupants traveled by the railroad from Norfolk . . . By the end of 1962, there were 8,718 residents in the tiny area incorporated as Virginia Beach, and 91,307 people in adjoining Princess Anne County. The two merged on Jan. 1, 1963 . . . The city has experi-*

*enced a tremendous population boom . . .
and the total figure is now almost 180,000.
The 50-mile-long city is known as the "world's
largest resort city" . . .* [By 1979, the city was
home to 250,000 residents and by the 1990
census, Virginia Beach had become the
most populated city in the state with approximately 350,000 residents.]

Report from *Virginian-Pilot,* Wednesday, 9/
03/80: *PORT'S TONNAGE MAY PASS N.Y.'s.—
Norfolk—The Virginia Port Authority predicted Tuesday that in 1980, for the first time,
the tonnage of goods shipped through Hamp-
ton Roads may equal or surpass the total
shipped by New York City-New Jersey, the East
Coast's largest port . . .*

A nineteen-year-old college student was interested in his future, and the line of work for which
he would be best suited. A portion of his reading
states:

*Case #1931-1*
Edgar Cayce: . . . In the present, then, as
indicated, the entity has the ability . . . to become a judge or a chooser of those influences for conservation—that *must* become
more and more a part of man's experience,
especially in the environ in which this entity
has come.

Hence, as indicated, the entity has a defi-
nite mission—not only in making for the
material gains for its own land and peoples
and nations, but to spiritualize those purposes also, rather than the conservation of
power or might without a channel or outlet
for the emotions of the spiritual nature of
man himself . . .

40

As to the abilities of the entity in the present, then, and that to which it may attain, and how:

As to the choice of how the entity will act itself, as to what is to be the choice of its ideals—that is alone to the entity.

For the urges and impulses may be magnified or minimized by the very power of the mind and impulse within itself.

As to whether it is to be for the fulfilling of that for which it entered, or for the glorifying of self or a cause or a purpose, or an individual, must be chosen by the entity.

In those fields of conservation, not only that is with government, with the activity of nations—whether it be of fishes in waters, birds of certain calibre or needs for food, or for the varied manners that they give protection to certain portions of the land, or timbers or the better conservation of soil for certain seeds or crops—all of these are the channels as we find in which the entity may find contentment and harmony, and the better outlet for fulfilling that purpose for which the entity entered this experience.

Ready for questions . . .

*(Q) How should I expend my energies . . . ?*

(A) Just as indicated. There have been and are in those fields especially the *attempt* of the Government to lay out plans whereby man may be taken from various portions of the land or environ where there is less opportunity; but *here* there is the taking of the activity of the raw and converting it into man's use! But man must learn—as the entity may particularly aid in—to conserve these very natures in *whatever portion* of the land he *already* resides! Of course, the land continues to grow—for it is God's footstool.

Man's abuse of same gives way to those things such that it becomes no longer productive. But if there is the conservation of its strength—the lands, the timbers, and God's creatures that manifest through same—it is a continuous thing. For "Ye grow in grace and in knowledge and in understanding" is applicable to man's secular life just as much as to his mental or spiritual.

More than thirty years later, a report was filed in the form of a questionnaire completed and returned by Mr. [1931]:

Report from General Questionnaire received regarding [1931-1], 2/28/72:
1. What jobs have you held since your reading? (In chronological order)
*Timber Cruiser, U.S. Forest Service, Ranger-Naturalist, U.S., National Park Service, U.S. Park Ranger, U.S. National Park Service, U.S. Game Management Agent, U.S. Fish & Wildlife Service*
2. Have you ever spoken with Edgar Cayce? (Yes) (No) *Yes.*
How well, if so, did you know him?
*Corresponded frequently while working for the U.S. Forest Service in Alaska as well as spoke to him at the June conferences at Virginia Beach and after life reading and check readings.*
3. Do you feel that Edgar Cayce's source of information depicted you accurately? *No doubt about it.*
4. At the time of the reading, did you have confidence in his counseling? (Yes) (No) *Yes.*
5. Do you feel that the reading helped you? How?
*By giving direction to natural urges. After fol-*

*lowing the advise in the readings I have been truly happy in my life's work. With Edgar Cayce's "road map" the journey has been great in the conservation field.*

6. As you look back, do you see patterns that were shown in the readings that you didn't see before? Please explain.

*No. I think everything mentioned in the readings was accurate in my case from the start. It was only a matter of getting on with life's work. At the time of the reading I knew the information was correct and nothing has changed my mind.*

In a number of readings, personal information inadvertently branched out into material that affected many more individuals than simply the questioner. For example, a forty-three-year-old realtor interested in commodity futures asked for a year-end weather forecast in August of 1926. The reply came:

*Case #195-32*

Edgar Cayce: . . . As for the weather conditions, and the effect same will produce on various portions of the earth's sphere, and this in its relation to the conditions in man's affairs: As has been oft given, Jupiter and Uranus influences in the affairs of the world appear the strongest on or about October 15th to 20th—when there may be expected in the minds, the actions—not only of individuals but in various quarters of the globe, destructive conditions as well as building. In the affairs of man many conditions will arise that will be very, very, strange to the world at present—in religion, in politics, in the moral conditions, and in the attempt to curb or to change such, see? For there will be set in motion [that indicating] when Prohibition will be lost in America, see? Violent wind storms—two earthquakes, one occurring in California, another in Japan—tidal waves following, one to the southern portion of the isles near Japan.

Report compiled by a geologist for the 195-32 case file: *The following excerpts are from the MONTHLY WEATHER REVIEW for October, 1926 (U.S. Weather Bureau, 1926): "October was an exceptionally stormy month and the number of days with gales was considerably above the normal over the greater part of the [North Atlantic] ocean. Several tropical disturbances occurred during the month, three of which were of slight intensity, but the storm that created such havoc in Cuba on the 20th was one of the most severe on record" (p. 435). In the vicinity of the Kuril Islands, "the westerly winds increased to hurricane force on the 14th and 15th . . . " Reports from ships in the vicinity of the Philippines Islands "indicate 3 and probably 4 violent storms [typhoons] during the early part of October, 1926 (p. 438). Reports of storms in the Southern Hemisphere for 1926 are difficult to obtain or lacking entirely. The closest one may come in most cases are the reports in the INDIA WEATHER REVIEW." This publication states (p. 110) that "a moderate storm occurred the 15th to the 18th of October in Andaman Sea." The California earthquake of October 22, 1926, was composed of three strong shocks . . . "the principal shocks were perceptible over probably 100,000 square miles" (U.S. Coast and Geodetic Survey, 1951, p. 26). The previous strong shock reported (ibid., p. 26) for California was on July 25,*

*1926, and the following strong shock was on January 1, 1927. Three earthquakes occurred in Japan on the 19th and 20th of October, 1926 (Anon., 1926, pp. 340-342), but these were not relatively strong shocks and, apparently, there were no "tidal waves following." If "southern portion of the isles near Japan" may be taken to mean the Solomon Islands, however, then consideration should be given to the shock of September 18, 1926, that produced a sea or "tidal" wave which "inundated the whole island of Kokomaruki and part of Guadalcanal" (Heck, 1947, p. 283).*

During the course of a physical reading given for an individual, the reading foresaw future medical advancements that might make diagnosis from a drop of blood a possibility. The reading was given in 1927—at the time, this information would have been considered the makings of science fiction:

Case #283-2
Edgar Cayce: . . . For, as is seen, there is no condition existent in a body that the reflection of same may not be traced in the blood supply, for not only does the blood stream carry the rebuilding forces to the body, it also takes the used forces and eliminates same through their proper channels in the various portions of the system. Hence we find red blood, white blood and lymph all carried in the veins. These are only separated by the very small portions that act as builders, strainers, destroyers, or resuscitating portions of the system—see? Hence there is ever seen in the blood stream the reflections or evidences of that condition being carried on in the physical body. The day may yet arrive when one may take a drop of blood

and diagnose the condition of any physical body.

Report from file [254-3]: *Twenty years later, Dr. Laurence H. Snyder of Ohio University, speaking at the New York Academy of Medicine, told a large audience: "It would be possible for me to take a drop of blood from each of you in the audience tonight; then five years later I could return here, gather you together and take another drop of blood. Without knowing the source of the bloods, I could then assign the correct sample to the proper person." This was a striking statement at that medical meeting; it gave some idea of the enormous gain in knowledge about human blood. It was also brought out that more facts had been gathered in the 48 months prior to that meeting than were collected in the previous 48 years. Yet Edgar Cayce, twenty years before, had predicted such a development.*

Report: 12/27/69 Clipping from Dallas News: *PINPRICK OF BLOOD TELLS ALL—NEW YORK (WMNS)—A single pinprick of blood can now yield as much medical information as an entire syringeful. At the moment, new "microchemical techniques" are used only for babies, whose blood supply is limited and precious, and only in certain pediatric centers. But Dr. Knud Engel of Babies Hospital, who helped develop the microchemical technique in Denmark, says the technique may become routine for babies and may spread to adults within five years. The conventional method of obtaining a blood sample involves tapping a vein in the elbow crease for a syringeful. Arteries must be punctured for special tests. Using the microchemical technique, a foot or a hand is warmed, which increases the arterial blood flow. When sophisticated, minia-*

*turized electronic equipment is used to analyze a pinprick of this blood, the results are as valid as for a large quantity of arterial blood, Dr. Engel says.*

As a means of demonstrating the wide variety of precognitive information provided by the Edgar Cayce readings, a selection of personal case histories are as follows:

In an early reading given in 1919 (4925-1), a pregnant woman was treated by a doctor for a disease she did not have. The treatment led to complications and eventually two operations performed by another surgeon. Despite the operations, the woman's health continued to decline. Three additional doctors were called in, all stating that the woman could not possibly live much longer and would die before giving birth—killing both mother and child. As a last resort, Edgar Cayce was contacted by the family. In the reading, he confirmed that it was too late to save the mother, but that she would live long enough to give birth to the child, and the child would survive. Cayce gave a prescription which immediately made the woman feel more comfortable. When the time finally came, a baby girl was born. The child was so small and frail that the doctors advised against wasting a name on the infant—it would surely die. However, their prognosis was incorrect. The mother lived ten days after giving birth, and the child grew to adulthood, eventually married, and had two daughters of her own.

In another case (3740-1), from 1923, a gentleman was alarmed to find his vision seriously declining. Concerned for his sight, he contacted Edgar Cayce. In the reading, Cayce stated that nerves to the eyes were being strangled but a complete healing could be achieved in just nineteen days. The procedure recommended by the readings was to be performed as soon as possible before serious and permanent damage occurred. Cayce advised surgery that was unheard of by the family's doctors. The reading gave instructions as to how the operation for the eyes was to occur through the individual's nostril! The doctors warned against taking such drastic measures and the recommendations were not followed. Less than two years later, the man was almost completely blind.

In 1926, a thirty-eight-year-old man was told that his present employer was dissatisfied with his performance, but not to worry—he would receive at least three business opportunities in the foreseeable future (779-15). Within a few days, he had received a letter from his present employer regarding his job performance as well as the predicted three job offers.

A thirty-six-year-old man—wondering if he would ever get married—was told that in his "fortieth year you should find a happy union in marriage" (3343-1). When he was forty he did get married—to a woman that he had not even known at the time the reading was given.

In September, 1933, a forty-year-old sales manager was told that Prohibition would be repealed "by the 7th of December" (257-121). On December 5, 1933, the Twenty-first Amendment was passed by a joint resolution of Congress

On January 24, 1935, in a brief side comment to case 270-33, Edgar Cayce predicted an illness for the king of England in the coming year. Although the Cayce family had no connection or contact with the king, it was later discovered that—despite medical advice to the contrary—King George V insisted on wintering in England. As a result, he succumbed to a chill and died on January 20, 1936.

Faced with the possibility of bankruptcy, a 69 year old man was concerned that his son's company would be sold at auction. The reading correctly predicted that the company would instead be taken over by another party. (Case 304-3)

Frequently, pregnant women asked Edgar Cayce when they could expect the birth of their children, and he told them. In a number of instances, at the parent's request, he named the sex, and in case 575-1, he told the date of birth, the sex, and the approximate weight of the infant.

A young widow, seeking assistance as to her proper line of work, was advised against riding, driving, or walking near railroad crossings for the next few months (771-1). A week later, the woman was driving her car down the street (near the train tracks) when suddenly a man drove through the railroad crossing and ran right into her car. Thankfully, neither the woman nor the driver of the other car were fatally injured.

In 1942, when ships, trains, and automobiles were the major modes of transportation, an individual asked about the future of the airplane. Cayce replied, "This, to be sure—air transportation—will become more and more the basis of *all* relationships with other nations, countries, as well as the internal or national activity" (416-17).

Parents of a *two-day*-old child were warned that their child could one day suffer an accident to his extremities (3069-1). Nearly four years later, one month before the boy's fourth birthday, he fell down on a back stairwell and cut an artery in his temple. Thankfully, the next-door neighbor, a doctor, arrived within seconds and quickly stitched the wound without anesthetic—for there wasn't enough time. The boy survived.

An extremely wealthy and prominent New York businessman obtained a reading for his health (1684-1). He was told that if he followed

49

the readings' suggestions for treatment, diet, and exercise, he would have "many years of useful service and activity." If he didn't follow the recommendations, he wouldn't live much longer. Even though a doctor agreed with Cayce's findings and wanted to follow the treatment, the businessman thought otherwise. Three months later, the man died.

A thirty-four-year-old New York investor was told (1416-1) that his greatest success would come in the field of travel, trade, or commerce—especially in tropical countries, specifically Brazil, Ceylon, India, or Persia. By 1962, the individual had become a U.S. Ambassador to Persia.

In terms of global events, the readings provided a number of predictions, as well. Within this information, again, individuals were reminded that nothing was fixed, and that they themselves had a tremendous impact upon shaping the course of their futures. Perhaps the most notable information in this regard is the readings' suggestion that the period between 1958-1998 would be one of great global transformation (3976-15, and others).

A number of individuals are familiar with the predictions Cayce made regarding potential "earth changes." Although there are less than twenty readings of this type, somehow this information has become more prominent than many other predictions. It is also easy to overlook humanity's co-creative involvement and the subsequent changing nature of any potential future. For example, a number of readings given in 1932 (3976-10, 311-8, and 5748-5) suggested that 1936 would be a year of major cataclysmic change. The irony of this date is that although none of the physical earthquakes predicted by the readings occurred, 1936 did mark the outbreak of civil war in Spain, a declaration of war between China and Japan, and Hitler's reoccupation of the Rhineland—events which many pinpoint as the impetus for the eventual outbreak of World War II. Since the year did result in many changes (as suggested by the readings), we could theorize that what Cayce had once foreseen in the vibrational future somehow took on a different manifestation. Rather than earthquakes, the changes expressed themselves in the affairs of humankind through the outbreak of war.

Other possible cataclysmic events foreseen by the readings included a shifting of the poles after the turn of the century (826-8), catastrophes for the western portion of America, upper Europe, and much of Japan (3976-15), and the disappearance [submergence?] of eastern New York (1152-1). However, all of these possibilities were changeable and could be avoided. From the perspective of the Edgar Cayce readings, rather than the occurrence of "earth changes," the period between 1958-1998 was primarily one which would lay the groundwork for a global community in which individuals would begin to realize their connection and interdependence upon one another. In other words, events on one side of the world could no longer be seen as separate and distant. In fact, the readings provide some inspiring insights into humanity's collective future. The attitude that Cayce suggested for those living in the transitional period or "changing times" was perhaps best expressed in the following: "Be *glad* you have the opportunity to be alive at this time, and to be a part of that preparation for the coming influences of a spiritual nature that *must* rule the world." (2376-3)

Cayce predicted that the time would come when every individual realized their responsibility toward one another. In time, we would all understand that with God as our Creator, we were all connected as brothers and sisters. What was important was not a matter of religion, rather it was an approach to spirituality that emphasized service, selflessness, and love toward one another. The readings advised, "Let that . . . be thy watchword, 'I am my brother's keeper' . . . be he black, white, gray or grizzled, be he young, be he Hottentot, or on the throne or in the president's chair. All that are in the earth today are thy brothers." (2780-3) One of the world affairs readings states:

*Case #3976-8*
Man's answer to everything has been *power*— Power of money, Power of position, Power of wealth, Power of this, that or the other. This has *never* been *God's* way, will never be God's way. Rather little by little, line upon line, here a little, there a little, each thinking rather of the other . . . *He* is thine neighbor, and thou must answer for him!

Cayce believed that these insights provided by his readings would " . . . change the thought of mankind in general in many directions." (254-37) In addition, he saw an alliance with Russia, freedom out of Communism, and spirituality out of China (3976-29). In 1944, when asked which religious thought would lead the world toward the greatest amount of spiritual light and understanding, the reply came simply that, "Thou shalt love the Lord thy God with all thine heart, thy neighbor *as* thyself!" (3976-8) Perhaps, more than anything else, this was the promise of the New Age.

In an effort to demonstrate the extensive documentation maintained by the Edgar Cayce Foundation, a majority of two case histories are presented. The first is the case of Fredrica Fields, a young woman whose talent with stained glass was accurately predicted in her reading. The second case is that of Colonel Starling—a White House secret service agent who wished to write a book about his experiences with five Presidents. Here are their stories, the readings, and the accompanying reports:

*The Case of Fredrica H. Fields—case #499-2*

Because of her parent's fascination with the work of Edgar Cayce, in 1934, a young woman named Fredrica procured a reading. Not showing much interest in the material herself, the reading was set aside. Years later she would tell a newspaper reporter, "at the time he did it, it meant nothing to me. It went in one ear and out the other." After the reading, time passed and Fredrica became a housewife and a mother—forgetting all about the information that had been given to her by Mr. Cayce. In fact, it was not until her mother died that Fredrica found the reading among some of her mother's personal papers. In 1977, Fredrica contacted the Cayce Foundation to inform them of the accuracy of what her reading had foretold. In part, her reading states:

> Edgar Cayce: . . . The influences from Mercury show the high mental abilities; with the Aquarian influence in its relationships to the Jupiterian making for abilities in certain given lines of activity. And these, as we find, will change, do change, as developments are applied in the experience of the entity in its relation to the active influences in the present sojourn. For, as in the present, certain types of art and its relationships to activities in individuals' lives may make for an influence

in the present activities. And there will come those periods when the activities in relation to art, that has to do with a great deal more of that as from stained glass or those that make for activities in the prism reactions to influences as related to things and to people, will be of a greater interest; as also music of a certain character or nature, or nature studies will become the more active in the experience of the entity as changes come . . .

Hence, the abilities in the present and that to which it may attain, and how, may be added also in these:

One having an analytical mind. One that may mete for individual activity much that may be helpful; for much may be given by the entity in its associations and relations among individuals.

And in those fields that are innately and manifestedly in the experience in the present, of the art, of the music, and especially that which may come in those that may make for the light through such activities to others, the entity may gain the knowledge of self—and in gaining the knowledge of self make applicable in the experience its relationships to others, thus bringing the greater development in this experience . . .

May the entity then in its own development find, and know through those things that have been given here, that in the study and in the application of same in the present experience may the entity come to know self better and in whom and in what it may believe. Seek; for only the seeker may find. Do not lose confidence in self. Know in what thou hast believed, and if it does not answer to that thou hast set as thine ideal—know it will turn to but clay, and thus only reach the satisfying of cravings. But let thine heart, thine mind, thine soul, be joyous in that thou hast gained in thine experience, that to express love in thine activities to thy neighbor is the greater service that a soul may give in this mundane sphere.

We are through for the present.

Report from [499], March, 1977: *Imagine my surprise to find the following in my Life Reading: "and there will come those periods when the activities in relation to art, that has to do with a great deal more of that as from stained glass" . . . I was deep in the study of stained glass, with a deep inner feeling that this was to be my life. Mr. Cayce went on to say music and nature would also be important to me. These three things—next to my family—are my life. I am enclosing a few papers for you in the hope they may be of interest because of the prophecy of what I would do. I thought there might be someone studying this aspect of the readings . . . It might also be of interest to you that I am self taught in the field of stained glass, and have developed this original approach on my own that is quite different from anyone else's work, either in the U.S. or Europe. A number of books and magazines have given space to my techniques.*

Fredrica Fields also reported that she had been a student of voice and ballet and that she could play the piano and the organ—in fact, she stated that she "could not live without music." She also tended a large garden in order to raise her own organic fruits and vegetables. In terms of her stained glass work, she had won awards at the Corcoran Gallery of Art and the National Collection of Fine Arts at the Smithsonian Institution. Because the reading so accurately depicted the individual she would become, in August, 1977, Fredrica and her husband, Brigadier General Kenneth E. Fields, visited the A.R.E. (Cayce Headquarters) in order to take measurements for the two sets of stained glass windows she wished to donate to the organization. When completed, each window consisted of three panels, measured twenty foot in length, and weighed 300 pounds. A headline from the 12/7/78 issue of *The Beacon* read: "Artist Fulfills Cayce Prediction."

In 1992, Fredrica died at the age of eighty. Her obituary is the final report in her case file:

*Fredrica H. Fields, 80, a nationally known and widely exhibited stained glass artist, died of natural causes March 4 at Greenwich Hospital. A resident of Greenwich for 33 years, she was creating stained glass windows up to the time of her death. Her most recent installations were two windows at The Church of the Holy Comforter in Kenilworth, Ill. Regarded as a pioneer and innovator in the field of abstract stained glass windows, Mrs. Fields received inquiries and requests for her windows from as far away as Saudi Arabia and India. While stained glass windows are usually associated with cathedral windows depicting biblical scenes, hers are abstract designs using layers of different types of glass of varied shapes and colors. Mrs. Fields had taught classes at the Greenwich YWCA and her work was shown in exhibits of The Greenwich Art Society and the Stamford Art Association. She was a member of the Stained Glass Association of America, from which she received several first-place commendations. Locations of her glass installations include the Greenwich YWCA, the Cole Auditorium of the Greenwich Library, St. John's Episcopal Church in Stamford, The National Cathedral in Washington, D.C., The Connecticut Hospice in Branford, Concordia College in Bronxville, N.Y., and the Association for Research and Enlightenment Meditation Center in Virginia Beach, VA. Additionally, her works are part of the permanent collection of glass at the Corning Museum in Corning, N.Y.*

*The Case of Colonel Starling—case #3182-1*

Colonel Edmund W. "Bill" Starling had been a secret service agent in the White House for nearly thirty years. During his career he had personally served five presidents (Wilson, Harding, Coolidge, Hoover, and Roosevelt). At sixty-seven, it was his desire to retire and to write a book which would detail his White House experiences. Seeking advice, he spoke to a personal friend, David Kahn, and asked for suggestions on the book project. For years, Kahn had been a supporter and enthusiast of the Edgar Cayce readings. It was Kahn who suggested that the Colonel obtain a reading.

In August of 1943, before the reading had been given, Thomas Sugrue, also a friend of Kahn's, expressed interest in the project. His enthusiasm comes through in the following letter, contained in the [3182] case file:

Letter from Thomas Sugrue to David E. Kahn: *This is the tale of one man's observation of the most important events in the history of man. When Starling went to the White House for his first assignment . . . the civilized world was largely lighted by kerosene and gas. Telephones were uncommon. Movies were, like airplanes, in the experimental stage. Radio was unknown. Democracies were the ex-*

*ception to the rule in government . . . etc. . . .
we give a picture of the world about to make
the big change . . . Often it has been said—"If
the walls could talk." Now here is a wall or
chair, or desk, as it were, which saw all of history unroll through the Presidents of the U.S.
. . . This wall now talks. Here is the story, the
intimate story, of these men—how they came
to office buoyant, strong, hopeful, full of faith
and determination—how they encountered
disappointment, tragedy, disillusion—how
they went from office broken, ready to die—
how the world rolled over them, a giant steam-
roller which they tried with their pitiful efforts
to steer away from the common people. It is
the story of man's fight against his own inclination to take the easy way—it is the record
of man's will, determination, prodigality, im-
morality, irresponsibility, and final achieve-
ment—told through its reflection in the
personification of the American man's character and thought—the White House . . .*

When the reading took place, five individuals
were present in the room: Edgar Cayce, Gertrude
Cayce, Gladys Davis, Colonel Starling, and David
Kahn. The suggestion was given:

Gertrude Cayce: You will have before you the
mental, spiritual and material development
of [3182] present in this room; also his associations and associates. The entity seeks advice and counsel . . .
Edgar Cayce: Yes, we have the body, the
enquiring mind, [3182] present in this room.
Ready for questions.
*(Q) Reference the publication of a book on
my life, activities and experience—please
give the plan which will tell a fascinating*

*story, of value and interest to the nation as a whole.*

(A) This would present a phase of human experience, a phase of human relationships that would be unique; not only fascinating but could, if properly written and presented, prove a helpful influence in the present emergencies; setting an example, an ideal, for many a young man, that would make such a life story most helpful to this day and age. For, it represents a unique experience in the history of the nation, and may be presented from an angle that will not only prove beneficial to post war experiences again but will clarify for many some of those experiences that have been in fear or doubt by some through many periods of development . . .

*Do not* present *any* political factions. For, as the entity in its abilities and in its activities acted—and is acting—in the capacity for the love of God and of country—and the man directing the affairs of a nation perchance using the opportunity—as observed by a servant of the people—to the glory of God. *That* is the manner of presentation of this entity's service to a nation . . .

*(Q) Who would be the best publisher to do the job?*

(A) As we find, a serial in such as Collier's; published by such as Simon & Schuster.

The reading then confirmed that Thomas Sugrue would be capable of working with Colonel Starling on the project and stated, "you will not find a better individual." A final suggestion was offered:

To be sure, there might be those who

would seek to inject—some publishers would ask for—sensation. That is *not* the order of the day. Throughout the whole experience of each administration from the beginning with Roosevelt to the end in another Roosevelt, there are human interest incidents. The greater human interest stories should be about that administration least understood. Clarify some in others; not as political issues or as of telling or indicating even State secrets of *any* nature. Then present the *great opportunity* of the American nation, and missing the boat—in the Peace Conference. These are the great themes, and those that—when the entity searches his own self—find the greater appeal to the inner man.

In other readings, Cayce had repeatedly stated that the United States had been remiss in not accepting Woodrow Wilson's plan for a League of Nations. After this gentle rebuff, additional advice was given, including the reminder that "no politics" were to be a part of the book. Colonel Starling then asked a final question:

*(Q) How much should be said of present-day visitors at White House known to me?*
(A) Enough to indicate the needs of the warnings. This is to the fellow man! not to laud any particular President, but principles—principles! Not to belittle any, as it will not be the purpose of the individual entity here presenting same; nor should it be sarcastic nor anything bordering upon same—by the one writing the story. The truth, sure—but *principle* first! And it will be, then, not merely a best seller but—for many years—the ideal of many an American.
We are through for the present.

Armed with the information that Sugrue was the proper writer, that Simon & Schuster should be approached about publication, and that the book would be "not merely a Best Seller but . . . the ideal of many an American," Colonel Starling returned to Washington and David Kahn headed home for New York. In an interview given in 1959 to *NBC's Monitor National Radio Show*, David Kahn described the next chain of events.

> *David Kahn: . . . I came onto New York and caught the only taxicab in Pennsylvania Station that was standing there at one o'clock in the morning . . . I looked over and saw a man in the back of the crowd with a big suitcase on his shoulder. I said, "You over there, with the big suitcase. Are you going up town?" I was embarrassed . . . all these people—one person, two people in a cab.*
>
> *"Sure," he said. "I'm going up town and I'd like to ride." I said, "Come on over."*
>
> *He gets in, puts down his coat, puts down his suitcase. He says, "Schuster's my name."*
>
> *I said, "You wouldn't be of Simon and Schuster?"*
>
> *He says, "I'm Maxwell Schuster."*
>
> *I said, "I'm David E. Kahn, and you're going to publish a book for me."*
>
> *He says, "What book?"*
>
> *I said, "Starling of the White House . . . "*

David Kahn proceeded to tell Mr. Schuster about the reading with Edgar Cayce. Later, a lunch meeting was arranged between Schuster, Kahn and Starling. Thomas Sugrue was hired to write the manuscript, and the book was eventually written. After publication, Maxwell Schuster occasionally referred to the book as "the Cayce book," and he gave an interview detailing the story of the ride in the cab with Kahn, the reading given by Cayce, and the success of the publication.

In September, 1943, the Norfolk *Ledger-Dispatch* featured an article "Presidential Protector to Retire":

*Washington, Sept. 20. (AP)—Col. Edmund W. (Big Bill) Starling, 67-year-old secret service veteran who helped guard five Presidents, will turn in his shooting irons around November 1 and retire to a less exciting life of fishing and hunting in Florida . . . Starling joined the secret service on November 14, 1914, during the first administration of Woodrow Wilson. He became supervising agent of the White House detail during the first term of Franklin D. Roosevelt, but turned over that title to a much younger man, Michael F. Reilly, about a year ago. Starling has traveled more than a million miles as a secret service man—with and in advance of traveling Presidents, investigating routes and arranging police protection for them. While retiring from government service, he says he will hold himself in readiness in event his services are needed for the American delegation to the next peace gathering. Although most of his 30 years as a secret service man were passed as a White House agent, Starling and his staff of husky young marksmen never have had to tangle with an attempted assassination in public. That, perhaps, explains secret service efficiency. Most of its work is preventive.*

Just as Cayce predicted, the book was published by Simon & Schuster. Unfortunately, neither Edgar Cayce nor Colonel Starling lived to see its release. In March, 1946, the Norfolk *Ledger-*

*Dispatch* featured a review of the book, *Starling of the White House,* under the heading, "He Guarded Presidents for 30 Years":

*There is nothing else in the whole world quite like the White House detail of the Secret Service. These men are primarily guardians of Presidents, and they have successfully prevented catastrophe for nearly half a century. But more than guardians: they are comrades to Presidents, they are diplomats, they are friends and confidants and they have helped to lighten the weary, lonely load of many a Chief Executive. Chief among these remarkable men, indeed, unique among them, was Col. Edmund W. Starling. I have never met a more engaging amiable, and utterly competent man. The first time I entered the White House, as a young reporter, I met him and immediately felt warmed by his welcome. And I was only one among many thousands in all parts of the United States who felt just the same way. But I did not need friends, and sometimes Presidents did, Colonel Starling was one of Calvin Coolidge's closest friends and companions. He taught the shy and stiff Vermonter to fish and humanized him perhaps more than anybody else ever did. He was deeply attached to Woodrow Wilson, although he spent many a cold night waiting on the sidewalk while President Wilson paid court to his second wife, Edith Bolling Galt. He felt a sympathy and pity for Warren Harding, and from direct observation he cleans up some lingering stains on President Harding's memory. Colonel Starling was not able to bring friendship to another lonely man; Herbert Hoover. And Franklin Roosevelt had many friends already, although he* *and Colonel Starling were very close. All this rich and important tapestry of memories is delightfully recorded in STARLING OF THE WHITE HOUSE, a book put together in Colonel Starling's own words by Thomas Sugrue, (New York: Simon and Schuster, $3). It tells more of two Presidents at least, Wilson and Coolidge, than most of their biographies. It is a priceless aid to the historian ...*

*The best stories are of Coolidge and Wilson. There is President Wilson walking down Connecticut Avenue dancing little jigs, after a courtship visit to Mrs. Galt, whistling: "Oh, you beautiful doll! You great big beautiful doll!" There is President Coolidge, asking Colonel Starling to lend him "ten." "Ten dollars?" asked Starling. "No, ten cents," said the President. Always, Colonel Starling's deep religious sense is apparent. And his great gentleness, as well as his extreme competence in his job. His sharp eyes saw everything that might endanger his Presidents. Yet best of all was not his negative job of protection, but his positive job of helping to enlighten and brighten the lives of these solitary leaders ...*

By June of 1946, *Starling of the White House* had sold more than one hundred thousand copies. Later, it became a book of the month club selection, and before it had gone out of print it would sell over 200,000 copies!

Repeatedly, the readings demonstrated the ability to perceive insights and information from the future with uncanny accuracy. In light of this amazing talent for seeing humanity's tomorrows, is it any surprise that Edgar Cayce could peer so readily into the past?

Chapter 4

# Retrocognition

While in the trance state, Edgar Cayce's ESP seemed equally adept at obtaining information from the present, the future, or the past. His ability to peer into the past with uncanny psychic accuracy was demonstrated repeatedly. Thousands of readings attest to the variety of material available in this manner: previous happenings in an individual's life, including accidents or forgotten traumas; ancient history, including the geological evolution of the planet and details of tribes and civilizations which antedate recorded history; even the previous lives of an individual. Sometimes historical information regarding the present-life history of an individual could be confirmed immediately. In the case of a fifty-seven-year-old man, Edgar Cayce began the reading with the curious statement "Nabisco—yes . . . " (4066-1). It was later discovered that "Nabisco" had been the man's childhood nickname.

At the beginning of each reading that dealt with the past, Cayce would often appear to focus in on specific incidents that occurred during the individual's present lifetime. One example comes from the reading given to a forty-four year old New York housewife in 1943:

*Case #3253-2*
Gertrude Cayce: You will give the relations of this entity and the universe, and the universal forces; giving the conditions which are as personalities, latent and exhibited in the present life; also the former appearances in the earth plane, giving time, place and the name, and that in each life which built or retarded the development for the entity; giving the abilities of the present entity, that to which it may attain, and how. You will answer the questions, as I ask them:

Edgar Cayce: [In going back over years from the present—"right pretty little girl— '10—had the measles—'13—'14—'16—first real love affair—]—etc." . . . [The reading went on to describe her emotional traits, her feelings, her desires, her dissatisfaction with life and her desire to be somewhere else, etc.]

Mrs. [3253] reports: *I do not recall the exact year I had measles, but I do remember having them. The reading was right about my first real love affair—at 16; it was right about my being emotional. I have a large circle of friends, although I make friends very slowly I always keep a friend once I have made a friendship. My biggest problem is being easily hurt. I'm trying hard to learn how to overcome this. It is so true about my being dissatisfied and the hurts that seem to come to me. I would always want to have a home, but feel such an urge to travel that I often feel such an unrest.*

In the life readings—those readings dealing with the subject of past lives—Edgar Cayce would go back over the years from the present experience, briefly mentioning the years back to the individual's birth. For example, in 1937, a life reading was given to a woman who had been born in 1883:

*Case #1479-1*
Edgar Cayce: [In going back over the years from the time the reading was given.] 1931—such a diffusion of interests!—'30, '29—'18—such anxieties!—'17—'98—yes, a change again in surroundings—'88—'83— How happy they were [parents] to have the entity! We have the record here of that entity now known as or called [1479].

Frequently, when providing medical information, Cayce would pinpoint the cause of a present difficulty to an injury the individual had received in the past.

*Case #85-1*
Edgar Cayce: . . . *in the nerve system,* in the cerebrospinal nerves, we find in the region of the 4th, 5th and 6th dorsal there has been at times back a lesion produced by subluxation of one of the dorsals themselves. The subluxation has in part been alleviated. While the strangulation to the sympathetic nerves of the secondary cardiac have not been relieved, this produces the choking as is produced in the bronchials and larynx, and the asthmatic condition as produced in lungs proper. This then becomes reflexly to the bronchials, throat and lungs. At such times we find the blood surcharged. As given, at such times we find the other organs

67

of the system become involved before or after through their cycle of functioning, as is produced by the overtaxed condition in the system.

Report from Mr. [257]'s letter: *Mr. [85's mother] received a reading from you for his mother today which was truly very wonderful. It checks absolutely and he tells me that his mother had an accident five years ago in which the top of her spine was injured, just below the neck. Your giving out all this without having seen her and without having any knowledge of the case makes it very wonderful indeed.*

All manner of information from the ancient to the recent past seemed available to him. For example, throughout the years he was giving readings, a number of individuals asked Edgar Cayce for insights and interpretations into their own dreams. Not only could the readings respond to this type of inquiry, but there were occasions when even the dreamer had forgotten information that had come from his or her own subconscious mind. From his trance state, Cayce knew whether or not a person had overlooked a portion of the dream, and it would be provided:

*Case #136-4*
A woman [Mrs. 136] submitted her dreams for interpretation: *Saturday morning, June 6 [1925], I dreamed I was on horseback and fell off. The same morning I dreamed of my father at home in New Orleans and awakened thinking of Cayce.*

Edgar Cayce: In the one of the horse and rider, as the messenger that comes to each and every individual, and the falling off the rejection of the message in this manner. In the second we again find correlations of mental and the subconscious forces with the dearer ones coming in that mental relation, with the awakening thought of that having heard, with the wonder of the interpretation of the rider. All dream is not given here, for the vision of the roadway, with the obstructions as seen, and the cause of the horse to shy causing rider to fall gives that of the conditions through which the mental forces must pass to reach the greater forces in an understanding manner. This very, very good.

The Cayce readings provide a wealth of insights into the ancient world. A twenty-six-year-old actress (case #2665-2) was told that in a former life she had made cave paintings in mounds located in the northwestern portion of New Mexico—and they continued to exist. In a number of readings, including #261-5, he made reference to an ancient Egyptian pyramid that had yet to be discovered. Additional readings on Egypt stated that a "Hall of Records" had been buried in the area of the Sphinx as an ancient time capsule of a long ago civilization and would be found when the time was right (case #378-16). More than simply discussing hidden archeological sights and uncovered records of forgotten civilizations, Edgar Cayce claimed that the history of humankind went back some 10 million years. Although much of this material may be impossible to verify, sometimes contemporary research finds evidence to confirm information given decades ago from Cayce's trance state. A number of readings discussed differences in the earth's surface in the ancient past. A few examples are as follows:

*Case #364-13*

Edgar Cayce: . . . The Nile entered into the Atlantic Ocean. What is now the Sahara was an inhabited land and very fertile. What is now the central portion of this country, or the Mississippi basin, was then all in the ocean; only the plateau was existent, or the regions that are now portions of Nevada, Utah and Arizona formed the greater part of what we know as the United States.

*Case #276-2*

Edgar Cayce: . . . In the one before this we find again in this same land now called Egypt (this before the mountains rose in the south, and when the waters called the Nile then emptied into what is *now* the Atlantic Ocean).

*Case #5748-6*

Edgar Cayce: . . . In those periods when the first change had come in the position of the land . . . when the Nile (or Nole, then) emptied into what is now the Atlantic Ocean, on the Congo end of the country. What is now as the Sahara was a fertile land . . .

As if to confirm some of the above, an article published in *Science* (August, 1986), reported that the Shuttle Imaging Radar from the Space Shuttle had discovered previously unknown river valleys beneath the driest part of the Sahara. Through satellite imaging and on-site archaeological investigations, it appeared as though the present day Nile had changed its course, once flowing across the Sahara, through Africa, and into the Atlantic Ocean! Only time will tell how many of the readings' historical claims will eventually be verified.

In a letter to a forty-one year old businessman who had shown an interest in Cayce's work, Edgar Cayce attempted to explain himself how he believed the mind worked. His own words may provide insights into how his talent for retrocognition was even possible:

> From Edgar Cayce's letter to Mr. [531]: . . . In our physical bodies we find that there are nerve centers running from every portion to the central nervous system—the brain. It is this central nervous system with which we PHYSICALLY make material manifestations. But MIND itself, or that portion of the soul mind with which we contemplate things, may work independently of the body. Just as, having been in a place we can imagine or visualize ourselves in that place again— without physically going to it. The mind goes, and with the memory it has can recall it to consciousness. It isn't the conscious mind that recalls. It's the conscious mind that made the record of the memory upon the soul mind. Do you see what I mean?

In 1935, a woman sought genealogical information and "family records" (case #863-1) regarding her father who was deceased. Although she knew her father had immigrated to America around 1889, she knew very little else about his background. The reading stated that according to Customs records, he had entered the United States in 1890. The reading provided the name of the ship upon which he had arrived, the ports of arrival and departure, and described additional family records which existed in a small church in Vienna, placed for safekeeping nearly half a century earlier in a small box, under the pulpit, within the altar.

In another instance, after being provided with the name and address of an individual in New York who wanted a reading (case #921-1), Cayce began with the statement: "Yes, we have been in this building before." The location was unfamiliar to the conscious Cayce and his office staff. However, later, after thorough checking, it did appear as though his unconscious mind may have "seen" the building before—twenty-eight years and thousands of readings earlier!

Beginning in 1923, when the concept became familiar to Edgar Cayce, the readings began delving into the subject of reincarnation, resulting in nearly 2,000 life readings. From Cayce's perspective, the past merely provided a framework of potentials and probabilities. An individual's choices, actions, and free will in the present determined his or her actual destiny.

Sometimes an individual would request a life reading as a means of discovering his or her innate talents and the occupation for which they might be best suited. A number of parents requested a life reading for their newborn infant, hoping to provide the child with appropriate training and guidance. On other occasions, individuals sought counsel in the life readings as a means of discovering the root cause of their unhappiness. The readings indicate that patterns established in past lives produced tendencies and probabilities in the present. Those patterns and tendencies must be faced—hopefully enabling the individual to become a better person in the process.

In case #1541-11, a woman with an extreme aversion to the Catholic Church was told that her feelings had resulted because of events she had experienced nearly two thousand years earlier. Cayce stated that she had taken part in disagreements that arose between the followers of Peter and those of Paul. Those disagreements had led to her present anger and animosity toward the organized Church. It was time, however, to let go of the past. Her reading encouraged her to condemn no one, learning instead to overcome this senseless antagonism. Apparently, she was given just that opportunity as her daughter later reported:

> Report: *My brother ... married a Catholic ... Mother was so distressed—said she would rather see her son dead than marry a Catholic. I do not recall many instances in Mother's life when she was more distressed. Later she became very close to [the brother's wife] in many ways, she had to admit that her good points were many, although she never has gotten over the deep feeling of prejudice toward the Catholic religion.*

In 1929, a life reading was requested for a one month old baby boy. As with other life readings, Cayce detailed the child's past lives which had the greatest bearing upon the present and would be most helpful in explaining to the parents the boy's abilities. The reading begins with those astrological influences which seem to have an influence upon this soul. A portion of the reading and later comments are as follows:

*Case #759-1*
Edgar Cayce: Yes, we have the entity and those relations with the universe and universal forces, as are latent in the present experience. In the entering, astronomically we find the entity coming under the influence of Aries, the Moon, Venus, Jupiter, Mercury, with adverse influences in Neptune and benevolent influence in Arcturus and in the

73

Uranian activities—especially as related to influences as come with Jupiter and Uranus when square with Venus, for we have an influence at the time that would be unusual as to Uranian, Jupiterian, and of Venus—for these are as *benevolent* influences for *this* entity. Being then out of the ordinary in the Uranian influence.

In the influences—these, as seen, may be given only as tendencies as may be builded in the present experience, and these may be altered or changed by the training or the environmental conditions, as well as the will of the entity. The *training* then, may be in accord with the tendencies and thus bring harmony, peace, and an influence worthwhile, or the entity may be trained in opposition to tendencies and bring consternation and troubled conditions in the entity's experience in the present earth's plane, even to the extent where there may be physical forces affected in the individual—as has often been pointed out.

Tendencies, then, as we find with this entity . . .

Those of the tendencies toward that of strong, healthy, bright, and toward that of the art and of the influences *of* art in the life. This, then, covering a vast field—and may be brought into any of the channels as would be in keeping with that of the tendency, especially of delving into wood and its relations with those of arts and those of the precious stones, and as related to the influence *of* such in the lives of individuals as are makers, keepers, or as those that are bringing about such changes in the material forces and conditions of the universe in its whole to such conditions. Then, training and keeping in such lines will bring to the body those of conditions that will be the more satisfactory in the present experience.

Those of which the body are to be warned and kept from:

Those of water and of influence—any influence—that water or waterways bring in the elements of the material experiences for the entity; though there will be the natural tendency to investigate such by the entity, and these should be gradually discouraged rather than assisted towards such. Not discouraged in the manner as forbidden; for to forbid a thing to the entity is to make it determine to know the end of that thought as is sought concerning same. Rather, then, by reason and by explanation of elements that are detrimental to the best interests *of* the body, so train as to keep these in the background, but not forbidden.

In the abilities of the entity, these may be seen from those influences as has been in the experiences through which the entity has passed—for the entity would make a *great* physician. In the appearances, then—

In the one before this we find in that period when the preparations were being made for revolution in the present abode of the entity, when there was the suasion from withdrawal, or the establishing of a liberty loving people into that of a oneness in purpose of *own* rule. The entity in the name Ivan Dorr. The entity then in that position of ruling those that were disabled in a physical and material sense in the land now about which the body has again entered, and in the heights as are above the city there may be seen evidences of this entity's labors in the physical sense—on the mounds above

RETROCOGNITION

the palisades. In the influence this has in the present experience, that tendency of the investigator as to intrinsic values and of intrinsic worth; yet not *always* measuring same by *material* worth. Get the variation! for this, as will be seen, will be an outstanding condition in the entity's development; that is, a busybody, an inquisitive body, but not one that may be termed a meddler into other peoples' affairs for the curiosity of the thing.

In the one before this we find in that period in the Roman rule when there were persecutions for the individuals who acclaimed the faith of the Nazarene. The entity then among those who were in power to administer the punishments meted out, and became a believer through the faith as shown by those so persecuted. Then in the name Eldoirn, and in the employ of the persecutor Nero. In this experience the entity gained through that of the ability to change the mind, and to act as the change would indicate in the physical and mental experiences of the body, *developing* high in this experience; and in the present there may be seen that of one determined and one set; one not loathful in activity or in mind, but one that should be trained rather to play as well as labor physically, for one in *this* development may become one-sided—without the proper guiding of a whole, full, oneness of purpose. In the influence as will be seen in the developing of the entity, one that will be set—yet will not be so set, unless improperly trained, as not to be able to be shown that one is ever in the state of development, or of growth, in mind as well as in body. One that may gain the inner knowledge of spiritual effects in the material plane and make physical application of same.

In the one before this we find in the rebuilding of the Holy City. The entity among those who ministered to the needs of the ailing and the sick, and was the physician in this period to Ezekiel—who led this return. In the name Zedkahi, and the entity gained and lost through this experience—gaining in the application of self to those who labored in the cause; losing in the selfish stand as taken against those who persecuted the builders—and brought to self condemnation for self in the attitude assumed. In the influence in the present experience, the tendency toward the desire to know as concerning physical ills—yet loath to give sufficient time to learn well. This, as seen, is as contradictory to some influences given. Hence that of the influence to guide in the moulding stage to where sincerity and purpose must be, one, and the full knowledge before the application can be that as a basis for full development.

In addition to providing counsel to the parents, the reading described the child's character traits and innate talents. Note that the information suggested he would make a "*great* physician" and then gives a past life in Jerusalem when he had been employed in that very occupation. At a later date, Edgar Cayce told the boy's parents that the child should not be forced in this direction, but instead encouraged if [759] did, in fact, show the intelligence and the inclination to become a doctor. With this in mind, subsequent reports prove extremely interesting:

Report from the boy's mother when [759]

was ten: . . . *I met three little girls on the train coming in Saturday and they told me that my son was very naughty—that he had operated on a [dead] squirrel that he had found in the woods and brought in the liver, heart and kidneys to show the class. Now the teacher has decided to get him a set of doctor's implements so he can operate on another squirrel in front of the class.*

Report from October 1939: *[759] was elected president of 500 student body—the student council.*

Report from father, November 1940: *[759] made the honor roll and newspaper at High School. [773] (our little baby) is secretary of the entire school executive council.*

Report when [759] was twelve: . . . *[He had] measles about two weeks ago. He looked it up and made the diagnosis himself, before the doctor came. He is definitely showing signs of physician tendencies . . .*

Subsequent reports state that [759] went to Harvard, interned at a large eastern hospital, specialized in psychiatry, and later became an outstanding physician in his field.

A forty-seven-year-old woman was told that she had been in and around Rome during the period when there were the persecutions of the Christians [case #541-1]. In a letter received shortly after her reading was given, the woman wondered whether this might be the cause of her childhood fear:

Report from [541]: *You state that during my Roman life I was among the persecuted Christians. Here is a strange thing: often I've looked for the why of it and now I wonder if this is it. From my early childhood I've had a horrible fear of lions and tigers. When circus parades were in town and everyone turned out to see them, my favorite sister always took me by the hand to see them. I loved her and wanted to be with her, but tho' I liked everything else and always wanted to see the parades, the minute the cages of lions and tigers came I began to cry—to be panic-stricken and beg to be taken home. Poor unselfish girl, she wasn't bothered by them, but home she took me. Always the same performance—I had to go, but the fright was too much for me; no one knew why. Once I ran from the animal tent at Ringling's Circus, a girl in my teens, leaving friends, when a lion roared. And always at intervals I've had dreadful nightmares, and dreams of lions after me—I'd be holding a door with what strength I had against a lion. This bothered me so that I never would read or see pictures of them if I could avoid it, because of the reaction. My sister said when she knew you were going to give me a reading, "Maybe you had an experience earlier with lions." When you wrote about the persecutions, I wondered if perhaps this explains the fear within. What do you think?*

Whenever he gave a reading, Edgar Cayce's primary goal was to provide individuals with material that would be helpful and practical in their everyday lives. This desire to be helpful was no less true in the retrocognitive information. Even as interesting as some of the historical information may be, the real question is 'was the life reading material helpful to those who received it?' Repeatedly, documentation within the Cayce files describes how the information helped them, turned their lives around, or even saved them from disaster. In one case [#2157-1], a young man sought help and direction in the form of a life reading. His parents later reported:

*He was floundering at 19—not knowing
what to make his life work. Background of
seafaring men—did not care to follow the sea
. . . As a result of the reading he took up aviation and was very successful from the start—
flew all through the war—was a flight engineer
on a B-24. Went into aviation after the war
and has made splendid headway in one of
the larger companies in the Midwest.*

What information had been so helpful to the
youth? In addition to confirming the young man's
adversity to "water, waterways, watercarriers,"
the reading discussed the young man's floundering and suggested an outlet different from the
rest of his family's. The young man also asked for
some "spiritual advice" which was given. A small
portion of his reading follows:

Edgar Cayce: . . . In giving the interpretations
of the records as we find them here, these
are chosen with the desire and purpose that
this may be a helpful experience for the entity.

For the entity, while in the material experiences accomplished a very great deal in
some phases of the activity, at times there
has been a lacking in those things as might
stabilize same.

Thus in the present we will find periods
when apparently there is failure to arrive at
those points of contact or conclusions as
desired. Yet if these are carried in the spiritual as well as the mental, the material im-
port and material application, there will
come those experiences wherein the entity
will again be quoted as an authority respecting phases of that which as we find will
prove the greater channel of activity of the

entity during this experience—aviation . . .

[2157's question]: *Any spiritual advice?*

(A): As indicated through the experiences and sojourns, those variations that have come in the astrological urges are from the lack of the spiritual application of the truths known. Do not make such a failure in this experience.

Sometimes information from the past came unexpectedly. In 1932, at the end of an emergency reading for a woman [Mrs. 1315] who had suffered a painful and sleepless night, Cayce did not come out of the trance state despite the suggestion given three times for him to wake up. Instead, somehow he became a witness to the events of the Last Supper, which the readings described. A later reading suggested that the spiritual attunement of those present made the experience possible:

*Case #5749-1*

Edgar Cayce: The Lord's Supper—here with the Master—see what they had for supper— boiled fish, rice, with leeks, wine, and loaf. One of the pitchers in which it was served was broken—the handle was broken, as was the lip to same.

The whole robe of the Master was not white, but pearl gray—all combined into one—the gift of Nicodemus to the Lord.

The better looking of the twelve, of course, was Judas, while the younger was John— oval face, dark hair, smooth face—only one with the short hair. Peter, the rough and ready—always that of very short beard, rough, and not altogether clean; while Andrew's is just the opposite—very sparse, but inclined to be long more on the side and under the chin—long on the upper lip—his robe was always near gray or black, while his clouts or breeches were striped; while those of Philip and Bartholomew were red and brown.

The Master's hair is 'most red, inclined to be curly in portions, yet not feminine or weak—*strong* with heavy piercing eyes that are blue or steel-gray.

His weight would be at least a hundred and seventy pounds. Long tapering fingers, nails well kept. Long nail, though, on the left little finger.

Merry—even in the hour of trial. Joke—even in the moment of betrayal.

The sack is empty. Judas departs.

The last is given of the wine and loaf, with which He gives the emblems that should be so dear to every follower of Him. Lays aside His robe, which is all of one piece—girds the towel about His waist, which is dressed with linen that is blue and white. Rolls back the folds, kneels first before John, James, then to Peter—who refuses.

Then the dissertation as to "He that would be the greatest would be servant of all."

The basin is taken as without handle, and is made of wood. The water is from the gherkins [gourds], that are in the wide-mouth Shibboleths [streams? Judges 12:6], that stand in the house of John's father, Zebedee.

And now comes "It is finished."

They sing the ninety-first Psalm—"He that dwelleth in the secret place of the Most High shall abide under the shadow of the Almighty. I will say of the Lord, He is my refuge and my fortress: my God; in Him will I trust."

He is the musician as well, for He uses the harp.

They leave for the garden.

82

Interestingly enough, thirty-two years later, in March 1964, *Woman's Life* magazine would print a "Letter to Tiberias" which was reported to have been written nearly 2,000 years earlier from a Roman citizen, Publius Lentulus, to his Emperor, Tiberias. The original letter remained in the Roman archives but had been translated. The account provided an amazingly similar description of Jesus to the one given by the readings thirty years earlier. It reads:

*There has appeared in Palestine a man who is still living and whose power is extraordinary. He has the title given him of Great Prophet, his disciples call him "Son of God." He raises the dead and heals all sorts of diseases. He is a tall, well-proportioned man, and there is an air of severity in his countenance which at once attracts the love and reverence of those who see him. His hair is the colour of new wine from the roots to the ears, and thence to the shoulders it is curled and falls down to the lowest part of them. Upon the forehead, it parts in two after the manner of Nazarenes. His forehead is flat and fair, his face without blemish or defect, and adorned with a graceful expression. His nose and mouth are very well proportioned, his beard is thick and the colour of his hair. His eyes are grey and extremely lively. In his reproofs, he is terrible, but in his exhortations and instructions, amiable and courteous. There is something wonderfully charming in this face with a mixture of gravity. He is never seen to laugh, but has been observed to weep. He is very straight in stature, his hands large and spreading, his arms are very beautiful. He talks little, but with a great quality and is the handsomest man in the world.*

Not everyone who received a life reading was immediately convinced of the accuracy of Cayce's retrocognitive information. One example is the case of a fourteen year old boy [641] who had been given the reading as a birthday present from his older sister. The reading stated that in past incarnations the boy had frequently been involved in the material and clothing business. It was in this very line of work, Cayce claimed, that the individual would have his greatest degree of financial success and positive business interactions with other people. However, nothing about the career even appealed to the youth. Even when he had become a young man, he still showed no interest.

*Case #641-1*
Reported dated 8/22/34: *At the age of twenty-one, Case [641]—was still working with the small-town newspaper, although he had risen to the position of assistant circulation manager. He was making only a moderate salary and was then the chief support of his mother and a younger sister; he reported that he had no opportunity to get into the line of work suggested by the reading and, besides, he could feel no special inclination or urge in that direction. It was hard for him to understand why the reading advised a life's work which had no appeal for him. However, he felt that he was at a standstill in his present position and saw no chance for advancement; consequently he was seeking a change of some kind.*

Seven years earlier, Cayce's reading had included the following information about his past, suggesting that it laid the groundwork for his potential future:

Edgar Cayce: . . . One that, then, without respect of will, finds these conditions as urges in the present experience:

One that will find the greater success, the greater development in the present experience, coming through that of association with peoples—in the condition of the *business* man, especially that as pertains to materials, clothing, or of such natures. These will be the natural trend and bent of the entity in its relations with individuals and things, for with that of the ability to make friends, and of the turn that is seen in the *nobleness* of purpose, this will offer the channel through which the greater development in the moral, the physical, the financial, the spiritual way, may come in this present experience. Hence the training that the entity should have under such conditions and relations should begin as soon as this may. Either by that of the gradual development into the association of, or to get—as it were—the correct groundwork for such a development . . .

In those experiences in the earth's plane, and the urges as are seen from same:

In the one before this we find in that period when the peoples in the land now known as France were near to the rebellion, in the period of Louis the 13th. The entity then among those who were as the escorts and protectors of that monarch, and was *especially* the one that chose for that ruler the dress or the change of apparel—though *not* in the capacity of the valet. *Rather* as one who set the styles for the peoples. In the name then Neil and the entity gained through this experience, giving of self in service in the way and manner as was in keeping with the period, and not acting in any manner other than that of the correct in mien and in position. The urge as is seen—particular with self as to dress, and the ability to well describe the dress of a whole room full of peoples, will the body [if the body will] set self or *think*, as it were, concerning same . . .

In the one before this we find in that period known as the division in the kingdom in the land now known as Egyptian. The entity then among those peoples that were of the native folk, yet the one that brought much comfort to many peoples in providing for the application of the truth as was given by those in rule so that the native understood the intent and purpose. Acting then in the capacity of the teacher, the minister, or the go-between between the priests of the day and the common people. Hence among those who first in the land took on especial class of raiment or garments to designate self from other peoples, being appointed or given this permission through those in power, both religious and political. In the name Isois, and there is seen yet among the Egyptian ruins or relics reference made to the entity's application of self to the peoples . . .

Interestingly enough, in the spring of 1939, Mr. [641] was visiting some friends of his sister in another city. For three generations, the entire family had been involved in the clothing and uniform business. Aware of Mr. Cayce and the information provided in [641]'s reading, the family offered him a job as a traveling salesman. Desiring a change of some kind, he decided to accept. The results were extremely gratifying. Even in the first year's time, his success was phenomenal. There seemed to be something very special about

[641]'s knack with other people. In fact, the family stated his talent was not matched by any of their other employees. For more than thirty years, until his retirement, he worked for the company and proved to be a great success. In fact, toward the end of his career he took on the responsibility of training salesmen for the national organization.

Cayce had done it again.

Chapter 5

# DREAMS, VISIONS, AND
# OTHER EXPERIENCES

In addition to the readings which seem to delve into the categories of telepathy, clairvoyance, precognition, and retrocognition, a number of experiences seem to require a category of their own. For the sake of simplicity, these have been labeled "dreams, visions, and other experiences."

The Edgar Cayce material places a great deal of emphasis on the importance of dreams. Each of us is much more aware of ourselves, our surroundings, even our relationships at a subconscious level than we can possibly imagine, and these insights can be tapped in the dream state. Apparently, there is nothing of significance that ever happens without it first being foreshadowed in a dream. The readings suggest that dreams are a purposeful experience and that, " . . . all visions and dreams are given for the benefit of the individual, would they but interpret them correctly . . . " (294-15)

Oftentimes, while in the trance state and giving a reading for someone else, Cayce would have a dream which he would describe upon awakening. Frequently, a reading would be procured at a later date to get a reading on the dream itself. On occasion, the reading would state that much more than simply a dream had occurred, the experience had been a "vision"—an actual experience with which a portion of Cayce's consciousness had been involved.

More than 100 of Cayce's personal dreams are contained within his case files. Of these, perhaps one of the most frequently discussed dreams is one in which he saw himself being born again in the year 2158 A.D. in a coastal town in Nebraska! In the dream, even though the date was hundreds of years in the future, records of Edgar Cayce's life and work continued to exist. The dream had occurred after a court date and an arrest in Detroit for "practicing medicine without a license." At the time of the dream, Cayce had been depressed and discouraged, wondering about the future of his work. A reading was given on the dream, stating that rather than being a literal prediction of catastrophe for the country, the experience was demonstrating the fact that his work was important, meaningful, and would survive:

*Case #294-189*
Edgar Cayce: . . . This then is the interpretation. As has been given, "Fear not." Keep the faith; for those that be with thee are greater than those that would hinder. Though the very heavens fall, though the earth shall be changed, though the heavens shall pass, the promises in Him are sure and will stand—as in that day—as the proof of thy activity in the lives and hearts of those of thy fellow man.

Another of Edgar Cayce's more notable dreams occurred repeatedly over the years. It was a dream which portrayed his entering into the trance state, traveling through the various levels of consciousness, arriving at the place which contained the akashic records, and being handed the particular information that he was seeking. While giving a lecture in 1933, Edgar Cayce described the experience:

From report file 294-19: . . . I see myself as a tiny dot out of my physical body, which lies inert before me. I find myself oppressed by darkness and there is a feeling of terrific loneliness. Suddenly, I am conscious of a white beam of light. As this tiny dot, I move upward following the light, knowing that I must follow it or be lost.

As I move along this path of light I gradually become conscious of various levels upon which there is movement. Upon the first levels there are vague, horrible shapes, grotesque forms such as one sees in nightmares. Passing on, there begin to appear on either side misshapen forms of human beings with some part of the body magnified. Again there is change and I become conscious of gray-hooded forms moving downward. Gradually, these become lighter in color. Then the direction changes and these forms move upward and the color of the robes grows rapidly lighter. Next, there begin to appear on either side vague outlines of houses, walls, trees, etc., but everything is motionless. As I pass on, there is more light and movement in what appear to be normal cities and towns. With the growth of movement I become conscious of sounds, at first indistinct rumblings, then music, laughter, and singing of birds. There is more and more light, the colors become very beautiful, and there is the sound of wonderful music. The houses are left behind, ahead there is only a blending of sound and color. Quite suddenly I come upon a hall of records. It is a hall without walls, without ceiling, but I am conscious of seeing an old man who hands me a large book, a record of the individual for whom I seek information.

A very practical dream experience (294-189, report 23) came as a result of Edgar Cayce suffering from a cough and cold. One night he had a dream which prescribed a cough medicine for him to take and gave the ingredients and appropriate measures for each: 4 tablespoons boiling water, 1 tablespoon honey, 1 tablespoon simple syrup, 10 drops glycerin, 2 drops creosote, 1 teaspoon syrup of horehound, 15 drops tolu in solution, 30 drops compound tincture benzoin, and 2 ounces of whiskey. The formula was prepared and his cough was relieved.

In a lengthy dream recorded from December 19, 1919, Cayce had an unusual experience. Later, he asked in a reading whether the experience had been a vision or a dream. The answer was that it contained elements of both:

Cayce's dream filed under 294-15, background report: *Scene 1:*  Apparently, there was spread before me all the graveyards in the world. I saw nothing save the abode of what we call the dead, in all portions of the world.

*Scene 2:*  Then, as the scene shifted, the graves seemed to be centered around India, and I was told by a voice somewhere, "Here you will know a man's religion by the manner in which his body has been disposed of."

*Scene 3:*  The scene then changed to France, and I saw the soldiers' graves, and among them the grave of 3 boys who had been in my S.S. [Sunday school] class. Then I saw the boys, not dead but alive. Each of them told me how they met their death; one in machine gun fire, another in the bursting of a shell, the other in the heavy artillery fire. Two gave me messages to tell their loved ones at home. They appeared much in the same way and manner as they did the day each came to bid me good-bye.

*Scene 4*: As the scene changed again, I apparently reasoned with myself, "This is what men call spiritualism. Can it be true? Are all those we call dead yet alive in some other plane of experience or existence? Could I see my own baby boy?" [A son, Milton Porter Cayce, had die shortly after birth.]

As if a canopy was raised, tier on tier of babies appeared. In the 3rd or 4th row from the top, to the side, I recognized my own child. He knew me, even as I knew him. He smiled his recognition, but no word of any kind passed.

*Scene 5:* The scene changed, and there appeared a lady friend who was being buried in the local cemetery during that self-same hour, one whom I had known very well and from whom I had purchased many flowers for distribution by the children in my S.S. classes. She talked with me about the changes that men call death, said that it was a real birth. Especially she spoke concerning the effect the gift of flowers had upon individuals, and how they should be given in life rather than at funerals or death. As to what they meant, and how they spoke to the invalid, the shut-ins, and meant so little to those that had passed from material to the spiritual plane. Then she said, "But to be material for the moment, some months ago someone left $2.50 with you for me. You are not aware of this having been done, and will find it in a drawer of your desk marked with the date it was paid, Aug. 8th, and there are 2 paper dollars with a 50-cent piece. See that my daughter receives this, for she will need it. Be patient with the children, they are gaining much."

*Scene 6:* Again the scene changed, and there appeared a man [4971] who had been a fellow officer for years in the church of which I was a member. He spoke of his son [228], who was a very close friend of mine, but was soon to return from the army, saying that he would no doubt return to his place in the local bank but advising that he rather accept the offer which would be made from a moving [movie] picture house. Then he spoke concerning the affairs of the church, and then I was physically conscious again.

Edgar Cayce's conscious report of the above experience:

*In regard to Scene 5:* I went to my office and looked in the drawer of the desk where I was told to look and sure enough there was the envelope that had been received on the 8th of August by one of the young ladies who had since left the [photography] studio (and this was in December).

*In regard to Scene 6:* The next day I had occasion to go to the bank and the young man, my friend, took my deposit. I asked when he returned, and he said last night. I asked if he expected to remain in the bank and he said he thought so. Then I told him I had something I would like to relate to him, and that he could act as he felt right. He came to the studio within the hour, and I related to him the whole experience. He told me that on his way home from Washington he had stopped in Atlanta, that he had been approached by a friend and asked to take the management of a moving picture theatre, but he had that morning mailed him a letter rejecting the offer, but that he would immediately wire him accepting it—which he did . . .

*In regard to Scenes 1 through 4:* This one thing I do know. I have traveled in many portions of the country, north, south, east, and west. There are few, if any, cemeteries, that do not appear familiar, so much so yet that when I see even a corner of one I can with a few minutes' reflection tell many intimate things about that particular cemetery.

Confirming the fact that the dead are still very much alive—simply in another plane of consciousness—Edgar Cayce related an experience he had once had with a woman *after* she had been dead for some fifteen years! (See background report on 1196-2):

Awoke one evening with a rapping on the window, realized it was some one, arose, slipped on my dressing gown, went to the window and asked who is it and a very distinct voice she answered, giving me her nick name, telling me she wished to talk with me, to come down and let her in, which I did. Talked with her just as would any friend, for an hour, a very natural voice. A very real personality. There are many questions I wonder that I did not ask . . . I might have thought this experience just a dream it was so real, except that the Secy. [secretary], here was still at work in the office here in the home, saw me go down, heard me open the door, and heard voices during the time she was here.

On another occasion, Edgar Cayce related an experience he had witnessed while giving a sermon to his Sunday school class at the Presbyterian Church. (See case file 294-155.) While he was speaking, he saw a number of robed figures enter the church and stand listening to his complete discourse. From their attire, he recognized them as members of the Jewish faith—no one else in the church saw them. A reading stated later that these individuals had simply been interested in his topic and they had come to hear the lecture—the vision was real.

Another vision occurred one day while Edgar Cayce was tending to his garden. An apparition appeared to him in the sky. The experience is related in case file 294-185:

I was in the garden here at work when I heard a noise like the noise of a swarm of bees. When I looked to see where they were, I saw that the noise came from a chariot in the air with 4 white horses and a driver. I did not see the face of the driver. The experience lasted only a few minutes. I was trying to persuade myself that it was not true, that it was only imagination, when I heard a voice saying, "Look behind you." I looked and beheld a man in armor, with a shield, a helmet, knee guards, a cape but no weapon of any kind. His countenance was like the light; his armor was as silver or aluminum. He raised his hand in salute and said, "The chariot of the Lord and the horsemen thereof." Then he disappeared. I was really weak, not from fright but from awe and wonder. It was a most beautiful experience and I hope I may be worthy of many more.

A reading confirmed that the experience had been a conscious vision and that it had occurred to demonstrate the ever-existent Presence of the Lord—even during those moments when Cayce felt "periods of oppression."

In 1926, Edgar Cayce had a personal experience—one of many—which confirmed for him the process of reincarnation. While giving a reading to an infant, Cayce stated that in the life just previous to the present, the child [318] had been "Thomas Cayce"—Edgar Cayce's little brother who had died when Edgar was only fifteen. Later, when a gentleman wrote Cayce asking for what evidence there was for reincarnation, Cayce related the story:

*Case file #2722-5*
Letter from Edgar Cayce to Mr. [4959]: . . . years ago, many years I had a little brother. He lived only a few months—his was the first time death touched me—and as the child I did not understand—who does? Save, "In the day ye eat there of ye shall surely die." Time went on eventually some theory that reincarnation was presented in the information. I prayed earnestly about same, asked to be shown the truth, earnestly, sincerely, and I believe God hears prayer. Eventually, I had a very good friend—we will say a Mr. [779] and his family—a wife [780], and three lovely children—he was in my S.S. class. He and each member of his family had more

than once come to the information for help—and apparently had gotten same . . . a boy [318] was born. They asked for a reading . . . [The child was confirmed to be Thomas Cayce. Edgar Cayce did not see him again until he was two-and-a-half years old.]

[At that time] He merely stood off and looked intently at me. Then, suddenly he rushed to me with his little face radiant and said, "Brother." What that did to me, [4959], can never tell any one! He at once began to beg me to take him home with me—that he belonged to me, that he didn't belong there. I had to leave while he was asleep—I could not interfere. I know he was there for a purpose, what Who knows did not see him again until he was past ten. Then was in the home again . . . When I went to leave, he was packed to leave with me without saying anything. Then I tried to talk with him, told him how necessary he was in that home and he must finish school there. He was resigned. Incredible story, [4959], but every word true, so help me GOD! Had you had that experience, what would you say? And that, my friend, is only one of hundreds have experienced in the last 15 years. No, no, no, not proof to anyone but mighty meaningful to me.

In addition to being able to give readings in the trance state, Edgar Cayce was extremely psychic in the waking state. One of his psychic talents was the ability to see "auras"—patterns of light which emanate from individuals and contain information regarding their health, their frame of mind, even events in their lives. As a demonstration of this perceptive ability, on the night of August 26, 1941, at his Tuesday night Bible class, Edgar

Cayce went around the room and described the auras of those in attendance (report file 5746-1). Although more than twenty people were present, only a few of the comments given that night to specific individuals are recorded here in order to give an indication of what took place:

[2533]: You have more violet in your aura than anyone in the room. Violet always indicates the seeker, the searcher for something. You have more of [violet] than gray, blue, opal, white or pink. A great deal of pink or coral in an individual's aura indicates material-mindedness.

[845]: You have a light more than you have an aura. There is a light that stays about you now, which may become a part of your aura or it may be a thing that you are attaining to. But there's more of a white light that stays about you as an aura. Not many people have a white light, because when most people attain to a white light they are getting ready to do something in the way of individual accomplishment; that is, it represents that surety in which an individual has put a hope—and such an environ is created about the individual. It is not a ball of light, but more a shaft of light—that with your dark hair appears to be almost white.

[404]: The last time I read your aura there were a lot of shadows about it. Now it is entirely different. I would see from your aura that you have some very unusual news coming to you. This is indicated by the way in which your aura circles about the head—a circle and one above it, and one above it; more like we usually picture a halo—a streak of gold, as that especially about a picture of the Master. There is gold

and white, which would indicate good news. [1523]: You have a very unusual sort of aura at present. There is a great deal of gray and blue and gold. Yours is mighty high sometimes and down mighty low at other times. It is very much like a crown, but a crown with spikes—a circular crown with spikes. Violet, opal, gray, and tipped off with gold. So at times you make snap judgments, at other times you give due consideration, at other times you don't give a cuss! This is indicated by the difference in the shading of the spikes; there are two shades of red, two shades of gray, two shades of blue—in those variations.

Although the vast majority of Edgar Cayce's psychic ability was demonstrated in the trance state, throughout his life he had conscious experiences that extended beyond the bounds of "normal" perception. In fact, these experiences had occurred all the way back to his childhood. Just as it is not unusual for children to believe they have invisible friends, Edgar Cayce was no exception. As an adult, he would occasionally speak about the "invisible playmates" he had seen as a child. One woman, Mrs. [464], had heard about these experiences, and the fact that Cayce had been called "a strange child" because of them. She had read a story about fairies (written by Sir Arthur Conan Doyle) to her daughter. When her daughter asked for more information, the woman wrote Cayce and asked if he wouldn't mind detailing some of his personal experiences. His letter follows:

DREAMS, VISIONS, AND OTHER EXPERIENCES

*Case #464-12*
Edgar Cayce's letter, 1/31/33: Yours of the 27th has been received. The questions you

ask are very interesting and, to me, very much worthwhile. All through the years I think I have been (possibly from necessity) quite a matter of fact individual. No doubt all my childhood and boyhood associates were also quite matter of fact. Consequently, I have gotten far away from many of the experiences that were very near and dear to me as a little child. As I look back upon the various experiences I rather persuade myself they have been steps in my development. Perhaps if I had paid more attention to them the present would be quite different.

I don't know whether or not I can give you sufficient insight to be worthwhile, as to just what took place during those experiences of my early childhood when I visited unseen playmates; for I will have to admit that—except for a general outline of my life, in which this subject is touched on just a little—I have never attempted to put those experiences in writing. So, if my letter appears somewhat disconnected or unreasonable, know that it is because of a physically developed body (and possibly a sane mind) attempting to keep within the bounds of reason. Except the fairy stories of Grimm and Hans [Christian] Andersen, I have never read of others' experiences. While I have had a little correspondence with Sir Arthur Conan Doyle, and have one or two of his books, I have not read the one you mention. I would love very much to read it, and will see if my son can obtain it from the Norfolk library.

These are at least some of my experiences. As to just what was the first experience, I don't know. The one that appears at present to be among the first, was when I was possibly eighteen or twenty months old. I had a playhouse in the back of an old garden, among the honeysuckle and other flowers. At that particular time much of this garden had grown up in tall reeds, as I remember. I had made a little shelter of the tops of the reeds, and had been assisted by an unseen playmate in weaving or fastening them together so they would form a shelter. On pretty days I played there. One afternoon my mother came down the garden walk calling me. My playmate (who appeared to me to be about the same size as myself) was with me. It had never occurred to me that he was not real, or that he wasn't one of the neighbors' children, until my mother spoke and asked me my playmate's name. I turned to ask him but he disappeared. For a time this disturbed my mother somewhat, and she questioned me at length. I remember crying because she had spied upon me several times, and each time the playmate would disappear.

About a year or eighteen months later, this was changed considerably—as to the number of playmates. We had moved to another country home. Here I had two favorite places where I played with these unseen people. One (very peculiarly) was in an old graveyard where the cedar trees had grown up. Under a cedar tree, whose limbs had grown very close to the ground, I made another little retreat, where—with these playmates—I gathered bits of colored glass, beautifully colored leaves and things of that nature from time to time. But, what disturbed me was that I didn't know where they came from nor why they left when some of my family approached. The other retreat

101

was a favorite old strawstack that I used to slide down. This was on the opposite side of the road (main highway) from where we lived, and in front of the house. The most outstanding experience (and one that I am sure disturbed her much) was when my mother looked out a window and saw children sliding down this strawstack with me. Of course, I had a lovely little retreat dug out under the side of the straw ring, in which we often sat and discussed the mighty problems of a three- or four-year-old child. As my mother looked out, she called to ask who were the children playing with me. I realized I didn't know their names. How were they dressed, you ask? There were boys and girls. It would be impossible (at this date) to describe their dress, figure or face, yet it didn't then—nor does it now—occur to me that they were any different from myself, except that they had the ability to appear or disappear as our moods changed. Just once I looked out the window from the house and saw the fairies there, beckoning me to come and play. That time also my mother saw them very plainly, but she didn't make any objection to my going out to play with them. This experience, as I remember now, lasted during a whole season—or summer.

A few years afterwards (when I had grown to be six or seven years old) our home was in a little wood. Here I learned to talk with the trees, or it appeared that they talked with me. I even yet hold that anyone may hear voices, apparently coming from a tree, if willing to choose a tree (a living tree, not a dead one) and sit against it for fifteen to twenty minutes each day (the same time each day) for twenty days. This was my experience. I chose a very lovely tree, and around it I played with my playmates that came (who then seemed very much smaller than I). We built a beautiful bower of hazelnut branches, redwood, dogwood and the like, with wild violets, Jack-in-the-Pulpit, and many of the wild mosses that seemed to be especially drawn to this particular little place where I met my friends to talk with— the little elves of the trees. How often this came, I don't know. We lived there for several years. It was there that I read the Bible through the first time, that I learned to pray, that I had many visions or experiences; not only of visioning the elves but what seemed to me to be the hosts that must have appeared to the people of old, as recorded in Genesis particularly. In this little bower there was never any intrusion from those outside. It was here that I read the first letter from a girlfriend. It was here that I went to pray when my grandmother died, whom I loved so dearly and who had meant so much to me. To describe these elves of the trees, the fairies of the woods, or—to me— the angels or hosts, with all their beautiful and glorious surroundings, would be almost a sacrilege. They have meant, and do yet, so very much to me that they are as rather the sacred experiences that we do not speak of—any more than we would of our first kiss, and the like. Why do I draw such comparisons? There are, no doubt, physical manifestations that are a counterpart or an expression of all the unseen forces about us, yet we have closed our eyes and our ears to the songs of the spheres, so that we are unable again to hear the voices or to see the forms take shape and minister—yea strengthen us—day by day!

Possibly there are many questions you would ask, as to what games we played. Those I played with at the haystack were different from those in the graveyard, or in the garden. Those I played with in the wood were different. They seemed to fit more often to what would interest or develop me. To say they planted the flowers or selected the bower, or the little cove in which my retreat was built, I don't think would be stretching it at all, or that they tended these or showed me—or talked to me of—their beauty. It was here that I first learned to read. Possibly the hosts on high gave me my first interpretation of that we call the Good Book. I do not think I am stretching my imagination when I say such a thing. We played the games of children, we played being sweethearts, we played being man and wife, we played being sisters and brothers, we played being visitors and preachers. We played being policemen and the culprits. We played being all the things that we knew about us. No, I never have any of these visions now, or—if any—very rarely . . .

But, as all such experiences, it was gradually explained away by our beautiful material-mindedness—saying it was nothing but imagination and the like. What it all means, I don't know that I can comprehend or understand. As I have said to you before, all manifestations must be of that divine influence or force we call God. All forms of life, seen and unseen, are essences and manifestations of that One. *He* would gather us together, as the Master said "even as a hen gathereth her chickens under her wing, but ye will not!" We are so cocksure of ourselves, we want to stand alone. Now, I hope all this reminiscing will at least be worthwhile. It is only my experience. I'm not asking anyone to believe it. We can't experience for another. We may only see the effects of what another has visioned or experienced, in the manner of life lived by another—and then judge by that which the individual has set as the standard . . .

We are having a lovely day here; it certainly makes me feel like getting out and digging in the earth—though it's a little bit damp yet, from our rain, wind and storm, for anything of the kind. Let us hear from you whenever you have the opportunity. Know that we are always anxious and glad to hear from you. We hope we may in some manner say something, do something, be something, that will give a little hope and help to you in some way or manner.

All send our kindest regards.

Sincerely, Edgar Cayce

On March 21, 1926, Edgar Cayce had a dream in which he saw himself scalding to death in a bath tub. A reading was given (294-70) in which Cayce suggested that the interpretation "first and foremost" had to do with "*physical* defects in the body that need physical attention." Later, the reading told Cayce that even after his death, his work would continue: " . . . the operation of the work, as is seen and carried on in this state, *will be* going just the same . . . " In addition to pointing out physical problems that he was then experiencing, could the dream have foretold his method of passing away twenty years later? When Edgar Cayce died on January 3, 1945, the cause diagnosed by the physician was "pulmonary edema"—water on the lungs.

# Conclusion

Throughout his life, Edgar Cayce demonstrated the uncanny ability to put his mind in a state of consciousness that extended far beyond ordinary sense perception. Over the years, his readings discussed an amazing 10,000 different subjects. Because of the vast scope of this material, it isn't possible to present a complete listing of all of Edgar Cayce's psychic experiences in one volume. However, all of the information remains open to the public for professional research or for more casual investigation.

Even today, many misperceptions exist regarding the nature of psychic information. Somehow the word "psychic" has been misunderstood to mean something out of the ordinary, something special, unusual, weird, or even infallible. None of these definitions correspond with the approach contained within the Edgar Cayce readings. To Cayce, psychic ability was a natural talent of the soul. From his perspective, we are not simply physical bodies, instead we are spiritual beings (with unbounded consciousness potential) who happen to be having a physical experience.

Psychic information is simply information that comes to us through our extended sense perception. In addition, it is not necessarily 100% accurate. We all have filters, biases, and misperceptions to which the information is subject. In fact, a book written by Cayce's own sons, *The Outer Limits of Edgar Cayce's Power*, attempted to explore this very phenomena in the Cayce readings.

For some reason, no one expects a talented business executive to *always* be correct when making his decisions, no one expects a good parent to *always* exercise perfect discipline or judgment, no one believes that a talented minister can *always* deliver an inspiring sermon every time he or she begins to speak, and yet, we expect something very different from individuals who call themselves psychic. Because of the misunderstanding of what psychic ability is (as well as what it is not), many people either disregard the information altogether, or they elevate it to an unreasonable level. From Cayce's perspective, we may wish to work with psychic information to the same degree that we would listen to the advise of a trusted friend. It can be utilized as an additional tool for gathering insights and for making decisions—it shouldn't necessarily be given any more credence than information from any of our other friends (or senses), however, it shouldn't be given any less credence either.

Edgar Cayce never tried to distinguish himself as the world's greatest psychic. In fact, his emphasis was not on the phenomena of the readings themselves, rather it was upon his desire to be helpful to people. The readings never offered a set of beliefs or principles that needed to be embraced or were necessarily infallible. Rather, they presented an approach in which each individual was encouraged to test the information in

CONCLUSION

his or her own life. With that in mind, the Association for Research and Enlightenment, Inc., was founded in 1931 as an association interested in facilitating personal inquiry and investigation into the Cayce material. That purpose continues to this day.

When Cayce was still alive, inquirers into his work received a bulletin entitled, "Edgar Cayce: His Life and Work." Contained within the booklet was a letter from Cayce, himself, which appropriately summed up Edgar Cayce's ESP. A portion of that letter read, as follows:

My friends, the life of a person endowed with such powers is not easy. For more than forty years now I have been giving readings for those who came seeking help. Thirty-five years ago the jeers, scorn and laughter were even louder than today. I have faced the laughter of ignorant crowds, the withering scorn or tabloid headlines, and the cold smirk of self-satisfied individuals. But I have also known the wordless happiness of little children who have been helped, the gratitude of fathers and mothers and friends. There are few mails that do not bring me expressions of appreciation for new life, new hope, new ability, stimulated through the readings which have been applied, in some individual's life. Trouble and worry and criticism mean very little at such times.

I believe that the attitude of the scientific world is gradually changing towards these subjects. Men in their respective fields are devoting time and effort to studying the laws that govern all kinds of psychic phenomena. Universities in this and other countries are carrying on advanced experiments. Psychical research must have open-minded, intelligent cooperation from scientists in many fields in order to be ultimately of lasting value in human experience. Our Association hopes to have some part in bringing about such cooperation.

There must be many questions in your mind, questions that can only be answered by a more thorough study of the readings themselves. Indeed, the final answers must come from your own experiences . . .

Under the Association for Research and Enlightenment, Inc., we are attempting to make a careful study of the phenomena of the readings and at the same time ever pass on to others that which is proven to be helpful in each member's experiences. I give myself to these studies and experiments knowing that many have been helped, and hoping that I may be a "channel of blessing" to each individual who comes with some physical, mental, or spiritual burden. This is my life.

*EDGAR CAYCE*
ca. 1942

CONCLUSION

## You Can Receive Books Like This One and Much, Much More

You can begin to receive books in the *A.R.E. Membership Series* and many more benefits by joining the nonprofit Association for Research and Enlightenment, Inc., as a Sponsoring or Life member.

The A.R.E. has a worldwide membership that receives a wide variety of study aids, all aimed at assisting individuals in their spiritual, mental, and physical growth.

Every member of A.R.E. receives a copy of *Venture Inward*, the organization's bimonthly magazine; an in-depth journal, *The New Millennium* on alternate months; opportunity to borrow, through the mail, from a collection of more than 500 files on medical and metaphysical subjects; access to one of the world's most complete libraries on metaphysical and spiritual subjects; and opportunities to participate in conferences, international tours, a retreat-camp for children and adults, and numerous nationwide volunteer activities.

In addition to the foregoing benefits, Sponsoring and Life members also receive at no charge three books each year in the *A.R.E. Membership Series.*

If you are interested in finding out more about membership in A.R.E. and the many benefits that can assist you on your path to fulfillment, you can easily contact the Membership Department by writing Membership, A.R.E., P.O. Box 595, Virginia Beach, VA 23451-0595 or by calling **1-800-333-4499** or faxing **1-757-422-4631**.